Creating a
Purposeful Life

Praise for *Creating a Purposeful Life*

Throw away all your other self-help books. *Creating a Purposeful Life* is all you need. Drawing on more than seventy years of lived wisdom, Fred Zirkle distills humor, grace, and hard-won perspective into a humble, heartfelt blueprint for genuine happiness. This isn't a learn today, forget tomorrow kind of book. His stories are engaging, uplifting, and deeply human—equal parts fun, moving, and memorable. By openly sharing both his triumphs and his stumbles, Fred shows us how much better life can be as we seek to "become" rather than to "acquire."

Michael McNevin, MD

Reading *Creating a Purposeful Life* feels like sitting across from a treasured and trusted friend, one who speaks with honesty, humility, and heart. Each page carries the quiet wisdom of a life deeply examined and generously shared. Through its timeless values and practical reflections, this book offers a gentle framework for living with intention, compassion, and inner clarity. It is both comforting and challenging in all the right ways, an invitation to live more fully, love more deeply, and grow with grace. A meaningful read for every generation: those we love, those we hope to love, and even those who stretch us into becoming better versions of ourselves.

Larry M. Mendenhall, former manager, Million Air, Provo

Fred's book provides a guide to how a person can refocus their life from looking inward to themselves to looking outward to others and thereby achieve a more fulfilling, purposeful life. He does this by reflecting on his own journey and transformation from inward seeking to outward enlightenment. By taking the time to read his book, you too can have the tools to transform yourself.

John Stern, Founder and President, Kentucky Wood Floors

I can honestly say I loved reading this book—the stories, the insights, and the profound life lessons it offers. I plan to use it as a weekly study guide to inspire changes and adjustments in my own journey with the hope that one day I, too, might hear those glorious words from my Savior: "Well done." Thank you for sharing your love, example, wisdom, and above all, your passion for continual growth. You've inspired me to believe, strive, and follow your example.

Mike Aitken, Founder and President, Crown Harvest

What an amazing work! I am moved by Fred's candor and humility and for the insight it gives to how he became the man he is. Since Fred guided my partners and I through the complexities of an ambitious business development effort, he has become a trusted business colleague and close friend. Despite being nicknamed "Mr. Irrelevant" in the NFL draft, Fred's impact on my life has been significant. His principled approach and character have influenced me to be a better person, and I am grateful for our association.

Chad Reid, Entrepreneur

Creating a Purposeful Life is a book that many seniors (myself included) will wish they had read decades ago. It is interesting, powerful and useful. The humility Fred displays in pointing out his foibles and mistakes keeps his prescription and advice from being preachy. Fred writes that it is never too late to craft a rich, balanced life, and his Three Levels of Awareness model helps set our sights higher, providing tools to facilitate our quest to achieve that life.

Steve Edison, Professor Emeritus, University of Arkansas at Little Rock

Fred Zirkle's *Creating a Purposeful Life* is a roadmap for business owners seeking meaning beyond success. His Three Levels of Awareness model offers practical wisdom to move from fear to love, aligning actions with values like integrity and compassion. This book is a must-read for those aiming to build a legacy of purpose, not just profit.

Cody Hilbun, Founder, Bespoke Capital Advisors

Creating a Purposeful Life

Awakening to Freedom
Through Values,
Emotional Mastery,
and Spiritual Clarity

FRED ZIRKLE

IndustryPro

Chandler, Arizona

Creating a Purposeful Life: Awakening to Freedom Through Values, Emotional Mastery, and Spiritual Clarity

Fred Zirkle

I/P IndustryPro

Chandler, Arizona

ISBNs:

Paperback: 978-1-971345-00-0

Hardcover: 978-1-971345-01-7

Ebook: 978-1-971345-02-4

Audiobook: 978-1-971345-03-1

Library of Congress Control Number: 2025927822

Edited by Melanie Mulhall, Dragonheart, www.TheDragonheart.com.

Design by Journey Bound Publishing

First Edition

To the many whose loving, moral compass set me on my purposeful path.

Contents

Foreword

I REMEMBER THE DAY, SOME forty years ago, when I met Fred Zirkle, his large, six-foot-five frame shivering and wrapped in a blanket from head to toe as he fought a fever. I wondered who he was and why he didn't go back to his hotel room and get some rest. Along with a few other executives from his company, Fred was attending a class on human values taught by my father, the late C. Kay Allen.

But Fred *could not* go back to his room. His body craved rest, but his soul hungered for more about the three levels of being and a set of human relations skills to live from: love, trust, purpose, and meaning.

Although a few hundred thousand people had heard my father speak or attended his classes, Fred could not get enough. He and my father forged a close friendship. The message about a new way of living and being resonated deeply within him, so Fred kept coming back (literally and metaphorically) to the Human Development Institute, the company my father and I cofounded.

There were times when Fred embodied the human relations skills we taught in daunting situations and better than anyone I knew—like when he quelled a mob of angry employees by listening deeply to their hurts and concerns and then leveled with them about the state of the business. He won them over.

And yet, I also watched Fred wrestle with how to integrate human values (compassion, equality, and forgiveness) into his personal and

xii   CREATING A PURPOSEFUL LIFE

professional life. He is ambitious, a doer. His natural instinct is to lead, achieve, and accomplish. I recall him telling me about workweeks of eighty to ninety hours in the early days of Key Tronic, the company his father started and which Fred led for many years. I couldn't imagine that kind of drive. But I also witnessed the heartache when things did not work out, his dream of transforming the company in ashes when his executive team wasn't pulling together, and when he was ultimately fired by the company board, led by his father.

I think about when his marriage ended and he felt lost and alone. Through deep soul-searching, not blame, he knew there was a better way and recommitted to his deepest values, knowing his journey was more about becoming than accolades and appearances.

As I look back today, I recognize an unrelenting refrain, sometimes subtle and sometimes clamorous, reverberating throughout Fred's life: There is a better way, and I want to live it.

Creating a Purposeful Life reveals this better way. From the moment I started reading until I finished the story, I was transfixed. Fred's raw transparency about the complexities, ups and downs, and successes and failures of his life reveal much about how each of us can live a purposeful, meaningful life. You'll come away from this beautifully written and engaging book enriched by the way Fred opens his heart and offers us a gift of insight into his voyage toward spiritual and emotional healing and maturation.

Something we have taught at HDI is that we don't grow from fear to a more loving and trusting way of living when life is easy. We mature and ultimately find meaning and joy when life is in our face, challenging us. Consciously or unconsciously, we make choices in these moments, and these choices shape us into the people we are today. Fred rightly teaches us that our values, if deeply internalized, are the moral compass that empowers us to make strengthening choices, grow into our higher selves, and find great purpose and meaning in the most challenging circumstances.

It has been my privilege to know Fred Zirkle, call him a friend, and be both inspired and tutored by his amazing journey. You, as reader, will no doubt also come away with greater courage and wisdom to live a rich and more balanced life.

Roger Kay Allen, Ph.D.
Cofounder, Human Development Institute
www.rogerkallen.com

Preface

IF YOU KNEW ME AS a young executive four decades ago, you might be surprised to see my name on a book titled *Creating a Purposeful Life: Awakening to Freedom Through Values, Emotional Mastery, and Spiritual Clarity.* And honestly, I wouldn't blame you.

You may remember me as a loud, demanding, and ambitious business leader oblivious to the feelings of those around me. The idea of living with purpose, guided by values and virtues rather than the bottom line, wasn't on my radar. So if this feels somewhat ironic or even hypocritical, I understand. In truth, I'm not proud of how I sometimes acted long ago. Back then, my passion overshadowed compassion. If my actions offended you or caused you harm, I sincerely ask for your forgiveness.

But life has a way of opening our eyes. Over time, my awareness grew as my focus shifted from *doing* to *being.* I came to understand and trust in God's plan for salvation, and that newfound awareness transformed me. Today, people and values come first, and thankfully, results are even better.

The insights I share in this book come from experience—lessons hard-earned and deeply felt. My hope is that they'll offer encouragement and guidance to you and those you care about as you pursue your own purposeful path.

Introduction

ONE EVENING, AS I WANDERED across the sprawling fourteen hundred acres of my northern Idaho ranch, I stopped to absorb the scene unfolding before me. The sun dipped low, casting a golden glow over the landscape. A gentle brook babbled nearby, carving a natural boundary between the thick green of the alfalfa fields and the tall cedars climbing the mountainside.

Far below, the first lights in the village twinkled to life while my herds of elk, buffalo, bighorn sheep, and deer bedded down for the night. Intent on independence, I'd built a custom home with a wood-burning furnace venting heat to every room and with its own water supply. It was an idyllic escape for my beautiful young family. Standing there enveloped by the tranquility and majesty of it all, I thought to myself, this is it. I've built the life I always wanted. The air was crisp, the silence profound, and for a moment, I felt wholly complete.

But then a wave of panic surged within me. A quiet, insistent voice whispered from deep inside. "Someday, you're going to die."

"I can't die," I replied mentally, almost defiantly. "Not now. Not when I've finally achieved everything I dreamed of."

Yet the voice pressed on, calm and unrelenting. "But you will die, eventually."

My mind raced. "Fine," I declared aloud, as if bargaining with fate. "I'll deed this ranch to become a protected green space, a paradise for visitors. People will remember me for it."

The voice responded with a wry edge, "Oh, so you need a monument to yourself, like the pharaohs of Egypt?"

That retort stopped me cold. Feeling a mix of distress, confusion, and a gnawing emptiness, I turned back toward the house. My boots crunched against the earth as I shook my head, muttering to myself, "There's got to be more to this puzzle." The beauty of the ranch, the satisfaction of my herds, and my pride in my hard-won haven suddenly felt insufficient. What was I missing? That question lingered, unresolved, as I retreated into the night.

A few months later, I recounted this unsettling experience to a friend and mentor. He listened intently, his eyes steady on mine, and then he posed a few questions that would alter the trajectory of my life. "Fred, what's your purpose? What gives your life meaning? What do you stand for?"

At thirty-two, I'd been riding high, convinced I'd conquered the world. His words knocked the wind out of me, toppling me from my self-assured perch. Purpose? Meaning?

These weren't concepts I'd spent much time thinking about. I'd been too busy building, achieving, and accumulating. His questions pierced through my self-congratulations and exposed a void I hadn't acknowledged. I was stumped for an answer. Never had I considered why I walked this earth or what kind of impact I wanted to leave. I thought about it, and after a few days, I wrote in my journal, "Purpose: to spend my energies understanding and striving to live as my Creator in order to eventually return and live with him." It was the beginning of a decades-long journey to realize my purpose and the values that would sustain it.

The ranch itself has a story tied to my family's legacy. I purchased it in 1976, a decision sparked by watching my father's first collapsed attempt at retirement. After a distinguished career, he'd stepped away from work only to find that a life of leisure was not for him. His restless energy and need to feel productive went unmet, and his discontent became a warning I couldn't ignore. When he fired me—yes, my own father let me go—I saw the ranch as more than a retreat. It was to be my avocation, a sanctuary that would sustain me when my own career inevitably shifted.

At first, the ranch was everything I'd hoped for. I threw myself into the physicality of it: operating bulldozers to sculpt lakes, cutting roads through the forest, driving the tractor as plowshares turned over dormant soil into neat, fertile rows. The smell of moist, fresh earth was intoxicating evidence of productivity. Alone in those fields, I began to understand the quiet wisdom of farmers, born from hours of uninterrupted thought amid nature's rhythms. The ranch was my paradise. We'd had our first child and my herds thrived. And yet, over time, a subtle discontent crept in. Riding through the valleys and forests, whether on horses or in vehicles, satisfied a boyhood dream, but my mind grew restless, craving greater challenges. I didn't fully grasp it, but I was yearning for something more, something beyond the pastoral idyll I'd created. I was seeking a purposeful life.

That ranch became my own first failed stab at retirement. Eventually, I let it go, drawn to a series of entrepreneurial ventures. This wasn't a random pivot. It was in my blood. My family's history is one of restless ambition and reinvention. In 1722, Heinrich Zirkle fled the devastation of Bavaria's religious wars. After losing his wife, he gathered his children and answered William Penn's call to move to America, carrying with him the Zirkle family crest, first recorded in 1603, depicting a resolute figure holding a compass. That image resonates with me: a symbol of an unwavering direction, a life driven by purpose and values. For us Zirkles, that compass isn't just heraldry, it's a call to live life with intention.

John Luther Zirkle, my great-grandfather, born in 1861, left Virginia's Shenandoah Valley to break ground on the frontier, farming ever westward until he reached Oklahoma. At forty-eight, he moved to Indiana, financially secure, and retired early to devote himself to his twin pillars of purpose: family and church.

His son, Sam (my grandfather), started as a farmhand at nineteen, later owned a bakery truck, then sold cars, and finally, in his late fifties, ran a gas station. Gramp's success owed much to his warm, affable personality and integrity, traits that drew a loyal circle of friends who'd linger at his service station, playing checkers and jumping to serve customers by washing windows, checking tires, and pumping gas.

After two decades, when the gas station started showing its age, Gramp turned down an offer from the fuel supplier, Sohio, to replace his station with a modern one. In response, Sohio built a shiny new station right across the road thinking they'd run my grandfather out of business. When I asked if he was worried about the competition, he nonchalantly shrugged it off. "Why worry? We carry on. Everything will work out." His customers stayed loyal, Sohio's flashy new place faltered, and within a year, the corporate behemoth came crawling back and asked Gramp to take it over. He closed his original station and made the move. His customers followed. Gramp's calm adherence to his values left a mark on me.

My father, Lew Zirkle, Sr., carved his own path. After twenty years at General Electric, where he earned a reputation as a turnaround wizard, he missed out on a big promotion and left to become CEO of Poly-Scientific, a small Virginia electronics firm. When the business was sold five years later, he walked away with a sizeable nest egg. A CEO job with Leviton (the company that probably manufactured the light switches on your walls) followed for a few years until C. P. Clare hired him in 1966 to run a small firm that manufactured illuminated switches in northern Idaho. I interned there before my junior year at Duke, helping design and install an inventory control process using new technology: a punch card computer system.

Eventually, Clare fired my dad, feeling that his efforts to grow the business exceeded his authority. His forced retirement floundered, prompting him to found Key Tronic, which became the world's principal manufacturer of keyboards. From him and Gramp, I inherited lessons in grit and vision.

In my business, which is helping people grow and sell their companies, I've racked up billions of dollars for dynamic, talented individuals. Take Robert, for example, who built a lucrative IT consulting firm over two decades of hard work. In his sixties, he opted to sell. After substantial research, we crafted a deal worth millions of dollars—enough for him to retire in grand style. He wanted to take a few days to talk it over with his wife. A week later, my team and I sat down with him again. He'd vetted our numbers, found them airtight, but seemed unsettled.

I'd seen this kind of hesitation before and asked what was on his mind. "I'm not sure exactly what I'd do with myself if I retired," he admitted. Work was his passion. It was his life.

Robert is not alone. After amassing fortunes, many entrepreneurs face an unsettling question: Is this it?

I now realize that life's final measure rests not so much on the things we've accomplished but who we have become and the bonds we formed with family, friends, community, and for believers, with God. Creating these bonds is not a retirement project. The bonds are important, and they demand lifelong tending. And the sooner we give them priority, the sooner our life becomes more rewarding.

A fulfilling life hinges on defining your ultimate self and the values to get there. *Becoming* is a journey, and as you find your moral compass, the journey becomes happier and more fruitful. Clients like Robert often sell their businesses and reap fortunes only to feel cheated as life wanes. They have a lot more money than they need but live with an absence of meaning. As vitality fades, if we cling to *doing*, neglecting *being*, we miss the intense joy of embodying our values. Life's richest rewards come not just from deeds, but from reflecting: What do I stand for, and am I living it?

Life throws challenges at us all: health struggles, financial woes, loneliness, stress, and even betrayal. How we handle these hurdles comes down to the sum of our experiences and how we process them. This book is here to guide you, no matter your age, toward a life of purpose and satisfaction by helping you define, refine, and stick to what matters most to you.

I've drawn inspiration from both religious and secular wisdom to offer practical advice. I'm a person of faith, which is a great resource, but you don't have to take my path. These are some truths most of us can agree on.

- Everyone has their own "religion," a personal code of beliefs and actions.
- We all have a conscience. Why else do we feel guilt after some choices and joy after others?
- Across major faiths and cultures, people tend to share:
  - Core values and virtues like humility, kindness, honesty, gratitude, forgiveness, and courage.
  - A sense that how we live on this earth shapes what comes next, whatever that may be.
  - The idea that good and evil forces tug at us, influencing our choices.
  - The reality that life's trials test our true values.
  - The belief that indifference and conflict wear us down while compassion and cooperation lift us up.
  - The notion that growing morally brings clarity and peace in this life.
  - The understanding that owning our mistakes, feeling regret, and seeking forgiveness helps us improve.

In the pages that follow, I will lay out some straightforward logic:
- Figure out where you're headed—who you want to be—and let your inner compass lead you.
- Living good values inspires others to do the same.

- Relationships thrive when you tend to them, not stomp on them.
- Hardships and temptations are lessons in disguise.
- Values mean nothing until you live them.

It's never too late to craft a rich, balanced life. Science backs this up. Brain plasticity means we can learn and adapt at any age. Forget the adage that old dogs can't learn new tricks. Humans can evolve at any time and at any age. The real snag isn't a lack of desire for a meaningful life, it's that daily grind that keeps us from pausing to reflect on our purpose. Work, duties, and busyness shove aside values, mindfulness, family, friends, hobbies, or just exploring for the fun of it.

Before I hit thirty-one, I chased whatever made me feel valued. In high school, I poured hours into training, earning all-American athlete honors. As a summer intern under my dad, I shone by rallying assembly workers, basking in his pride. I was humble and developed great relationships. When my dad started Key Tronic, he brought me on board because of my people skills, and we scaled from six to fourteen hundred employees.

But somewhere in that whirlwind, I let Dad and myself down. I lost that human touch. Obsessed with fixing problems and driving growth, I stopped seeing the people behind the tasks. How did that happen? Duke's football roster described Fred Zirkle as a gentleman. That may have been true, but "Gentleman Fred" wasn't getting much game time. So I became tougher and more aggressive. It worked well on the football field but not so well when I went back into the business environment.

Earlier, I'd floundered at Duke University, dropping out with no direction or achievements. Coming back, I was determined to stand out. I made the dean's list, captained the football team, earned the most inspirational player designation, and even got picked in the NFL draft. (Dead last, mind you, going from most inspirational to Mr. Irrelevant.) Those wins felt good then, but they weren't tied to a deeper purpose. I was chasing personal wins, not a life rooted in something bigger. That would come later, after plenty of stumbles.

As I completed writing this book, it seemed the entire world was in conflict. While 76 percent of the global population (according to Pew

Research Center) profess affiliation to faiths that promote peace, humility, charity, and respect for the individual, many people have set aside those values. Whether nations at war or petty local disputes, the language of disagreement has become louder and more vicious. Gridlock, bickering, and polarization have become the norm.

Ever-present contention inspired Utah Governor Spencer Cox to launch the Disagree Better initiative when he was chair of the National Governors Association. As he said, "Disagreeing better isn't just about being nicer to one another—it's about finding a way to disagree that moves us toward solutions rather than deepening divides. No one ever changed someone's mind by attacking them."

Governor Cox's call for civility in a polarized country gave him the national spotlight after the assassination of Charlie Kirk. "We just need every single person in this country to think about where we are and where we want to be. To ask ourselves, 'Is this it? Is this what 250 years has wrought on us?'" he said in an interview after the murder. He prayed that "all of us will try to find a way to stop hating our fellow Americans."

I agree with Governor Cox. We are becoming a civilization of reactors. Political division, social media outrage, and cultural tribalism fuel emotional impulsiveness, not reflection on morals. We argue defensively, seeking to find fault rather than reaching solutions based on our values. When driven by fear, pride, or anger, even good people become combative. We even stop talking to family members. We post before we think. Emotions and personal gain drive our decisions. And we start to believe the lie that victory in the public square is more important than peace in the private soul. The world is full of people standing for causes, but few standing in values. This is a root cause of personal misery, relational breakdown, and even national instability.

The time for creating and living a purposeful life and making a positive contribution to society is now. But why listen to me? I've found that success in developing a meaningful existence isn't about dodging mistakes, it's about learning from them and coming out stronger. I drifted too long, like a boat on stormy seas with plenty of thrust but no rudder. I want to spare you some of that drifting. In these pages, I blend my own story, flaws and all, with insights from wise minds and with spiritual truths to offer a roadmap for a purposeful life. You'll find lessons from my missteps, observations, and growth plus tools to sidestep destructive habits we fall into when we're stressed or wronged. One standout is the Three Levels of Awareness model—a game changer for taking control of your life.

Let me be clear. I'm not here to prescribe *your* purpose. That's an intensely personal discovery, unique to each of us. This book is for anyone, at any age, who wants to make the most of each day and in their later years, look back with satisfaction at who they've become and the relationships they've nurtured.

Constantly check your progress. It's how you stay on track. I owe much of what I've achieved through this habit of review, not through some particular brilliance or special talent. I trust that my experience and advice will help you nail down your purpose and values, paving the way for a life full of joy, meaningful relationships, and a higher purpose.

1

Why Have a Purpose?

WHAT DOES IT MEAN TO have a purpose in life? Why is it essential? How does it make a difference for you and those you love? Imagine purpose as a compass, a steady guide that not only steers you through the chaos of stormy seas but also through the stillness of unknown waters. Your purpose is not just a vague notion. It's a vibrant force, a mission that sharpens your decisions, roots your values, and gives your existence a resounding *why*. Purpose doesn't merely dictate how you move through the world, it fundamentally shapes how you perceive, react, and prioritize your life.

Think of waking each day with a vivid sense of direction, a clear answer to the question, "What am I here to do?" That understanding lifts your mental and emotional health and ties you to a cause greater than yourself. Across spiritual traditions, purpose takes on weighty dimensions. For Christians, it's submitting to God's will and internalizing the teachings of Jesus. In Buddhism, it's the pursuit of enlightenment, a journey to ease suffering for oneself and others. Far beyond fleeting achievements or job titles, purpose connects you to a higher calling—one that transcends the daily slog and often weaves in a thread of selflessness. Serving others or strengthening your community not only enriches those around you but also boosts your own joy and meaning.

Not everyone sees the point. Some drift through life chasing instant thrills: endlessly scrolling through their social media feeds, setting new records, enjoying the rush of the moment. They curate a polished snapshot of "the good life," but beneath the gloss, a quiet emptiness often lurks. And that high-octane aimless life has an expiration date. Without a purpose, life starts to blur. Days melt into one another, steps lose their purpose, and what once felt like freedom now feels shallow. The *how* and *what* of living grow hollow when there's no *why* to hold them together.

Relationships feel the strain too. Without a charted way forward, bonds can turn transactional or fade into superficial exchanges. Even surrounded by loved ones, a subtle isolation can seep in when there's no common dream to chase. The glitzy appeal of a purpose-free existence stacked with cash, status, a thousand and one social media interactions, or parties on the calendar starts to crack. Without a North Star, victories lose their shine, setbacks hit harder, and a restless itch takes root. Joy doesn't disappear, but it thins out, like a quick snack that temporarily fills a need but leaves you hungry and craving something more substantial.

In his *New York Times* bestseller *The Collapse of Parenting*, Dr. Leonard Sax describes a formula for living that many Americans have imparted to their children since World War II. It includes an emphasis on getting a first-rate education as the route to wealth and a good life. That goal, according to a Pew Research survey, was held by 88 percent of moms and dads while 46 percent said getting married or having kids was of little consequence. The result, writes Sax, is that parents promoting financial success and comfort as the primary worthy goals in life are promoting a life devoid of meaning.

This pursuit of a hollow ideal leaves a void that mere achievement cannot fill, pushing both parents and children to confront a more acute need. Beyond the chase for wealth and comfort lies a fundamental human longing for purpose, the guiding force that not only gives life meaning but also determines who we become.

Inevitably, the big questions surface: What's it all for? What's the point? What am I doing? Why am I even here? Finding purpose answers those questions. It's the difference between skimming across life's surface and plunging into its depths of richness. More than a roadmap, purpose influences who you grow into along the way—a unique quest that's yours alone to uncover. From ancient philosophers to modern psychologists, the case for a purpose-driven life has echoed through time. It's ancient wisdom reinforced by scientific studies.

THE FEEL-GOOD FACTOR

Research paints a striking picture: Purpose isn't just a nice idea, it's a mental health powerhouse. A landmark study in *The Journal of Clinical Psychiatry* found that people with a strong sense of purpose are less likely to grapple with disorders such as anxiety or depression. That stability does more than help you cope. It builds resilience, turning challenges into chances to grow.

A BOOST FOR BODY AND SOUL

The benefits don't stop at the mind. Purpose is also a gift to your physical health. Studies like those from the Harvard T. H. Chan School of Public Health show that purpose-driven people have lower risks of heart disease and other major illnesses. And they live longer. An analysis in the American Medical Association publication *JAMA Network Open*, which tracked nearly seven thousand participants, tied those who had purpose to a longer life. Why? Researchers say it's likely the result of better stress management, fewer destructive habits, and a natural desire to care for oneself. Purpose adds years and vitality.

RIPPLES OF GOOD

Purpose isn't a solo act. Living with purpose doesn't just enhance your own life, it lifts the world around you. Those who live with intention often pour energy into their communities, volunteering time and talent, which create a virtuous loop. It helps others sharpen their own sense of meaning, fueling personal fulfillment while boosting connection. It's a quiet revolution, one act of service at a time.

STAYING SHARP AS YOU AGE

Even as the years pile up, purpose keeps you sharp. Older adults with a clear *why* show slower physical decline and lower rates of Alzheimer's and other cognitive challenges. Staying engaged—pursuing goals, nurturing aspirations, flexing your mind—can keep you vibrant long after others slip into a sedentary lifestyle. It's not just about living longer. It's about living *well*.

FINDING YOUR NORTH STAR

So how do you unearth your purpose? The first step is to identify your central values, the foundational principles you'd stake your life on. What matters most to you? What ideals will form your days? As you navigate life's inevitable trials, holding fast to these truths begins to define you. You evolve into the truest, best version of yourself, not tethered to a job or role but to a deeper identity. Along the way, you might choose a career path—perhaps as a teacher, tradesperson, executive, artist, athlete, homemaker, or any other worthy pursuit—but that doesn't determine your identity.

A career might dictate your days, consuming your thoughts and time and satisfying ambition. But who you *are* is yours to craft and is entirely in your hands. Living your values and inching toward the person you want to be is a daily practice. Adhering to values builds a quiet, unshakable strength. With a clear vision of who you're becoming, you're far more likely to arrive there than if you drift between momentary whims. The life you live reflects the thought you invest in it.

This isn't about rigidity. Spontaneity has its place. Obsessing over every detail can backfire. Overplanning can cause analysis paralysis, trapping you in prep mode instead of action mode. The beauty of a purposeful life lies in its balance. It's a steady hand on the helm, not a locked itinerary. You take charge of your route, pushing through setbacks with choices that reflect your being and weathering life's inevitable storms. Purpose keeps you from being tossed adrift.

LESSONS FROM THE ROAD

I learned a lot about finding purpose in my own life through my relationship with my father, both personally and professionally. Family businesses have a way of revealing people's strengths and flaws, and the highs and lows Dad and I encountered were not unusual. Working together distilled strengths and struggles for both of us. Like many, he tied much of his purpose and his worth to his work, something that was common for his generation. In that culture, working long hours to provide for the family was a badge of honor. Work was seen as their purpose.

Because so much of his identity was tightly woven into his career, retirement hit Dad hard. I'm sure he would have said family came first during his working years, but nevertheless, he tumbled into an unbalanced life due to perceived work demands. It would be easy to criticize his devotion to work, sometimes at the expense of family life and other interests, but that is not my intent. I have always loved and revered him. So I won't judge—especially since I've mirrored those habits myself, influenced no doubt by his example and my own drive. Still, one of Dad's greatest attributes was that work wasn't just about achieving success and making money. He lifted others up, going out of his way to mentor colleagues and aid the less fortunate.

Today we talk more about a work-life balance than they did back then. Of course, work is still a necessity. We work to sustain our standard of living and care for our loved ones. Bills don't pay themselves. But it's rarely the purpose itself. Our values must be our constant companion. Sticking to your principles keeps you grounded, effective, and true, no matter the task.

A TURNING POINT

Prior to my internship with Dad, I was floundering. College wasn't clicking. I nearly flunked out of Duke due to lack of motivation, discipline, and undiagnosed ADHD. My performance on the football field was lacking as well. I had left behind what humility and compassion I'd had in high school and began partying to fit in with other students. I did feel hypocritical, but my attitude was "do what works for now." Seeking a fresh start, I bolted to West Virginia, where hardly anyone knew me or had expectations of me. On the way, I stopped at Bethany College to join my parents for my sister Irene's graduation. Her then husband, who was training to become a preacher, promised to catch fresh fish for dinner. And sure enough, he arrived home carrying a bucket overflowing with them.

"How'd you manage to catch so many?" I asked.

He smiled. "Easy. I dumped a bag of fertilizer into the pond. Killed 'em all and scooped up the biggest floating on the surface." His approach said plenty about his values, and it didn't surprise me that he never became a preacher.

Disappointed that I'd ditched Duke, Dad barely spoke to me, but I asked if he wanted to hear my plan. Without even looking at me, he said softly, "Nope. You're on your own now." He knew I had no real direction and needed to soul search to find my purpose.

I landed in the small town of Chester, tucked in the northern tip of West Virginia, and picked up carpentry work and jobs operating heavy equipment. Across the Ohio River Bridge lay East Liverpool, Ohio, a hotspot for Pittsburgh and Youngstown party people. The local police turned a blind eye to infringements of laws relating to the use of alcohol, and off-duty cops themselves frequented the bars. One night, after a delightful dinner with my date, we came across a parking lot brawl. Three bouncers were mercilessly pounding a lone guy. I hustled my date to the car, instructed her to lock the doors until I returned, and stepped into the fray.

Normally, even though I was a big guy and well able to take care of myself, I avoided fights. But I couldn't ignore such an unfair beatdown. One of the attackers leapt from the hood of a car and smashed the man from behind with brass knuckles. The victim's knees buckled as he slumped to the ground while others kicked him. I had to do something. I stepped in, broke up the fight, and helped the battered man to his feet. The club owner suddenly appeared and offered me a bouncer gig on the spot. But the brutes I'd just dealt with were his crew. "I don't want anything to do with their kind," I said, nodding my head in the direction of the attackers.

"That's exactly why I need you. You can clean up my place. Good pay, free food, free drinks."

It was enough temptation for me to change my mind. I signed on.

I started the next night, and to get a feel for the place, I showed up early. I'd never worked security before, but I knew how fights break out and drain the energy from a club. Intent on nipping trouble in the bud, I scoped out the exits I could "escort" troublemakers to. I was replacing two of three bouncers and hoped the one staying on would be a hulking figure. Instead, a curly-haired, Italian-accented man named Tony walked in. He was a wiry five foot six.

Nevertheless, I wasn't fazed. Sports had taught me that smaller, scrappy guys often did the most damage. Besides, at that age, I was an overconfident risk-taker who felt indestructible.

Tony quickly proved his worth, warning the regulars, most of whom he knew, not to mess with me if they valued their health. Still, there were some tense moments. One time I wrestled a sawed-off shotgun from a rowdy patron's grip. A girl tipped me off that a guy she'd been dancing with might have a gun hidden inside his leather coat, and when I confronted him, he backed off, arms held high before dropping them as if to grab something inside his coat. Taking no chances, I slammed my forearm under his chin, pinned him against the wall, and yanked out the sawed-off shotgun. I escorted him outside, and we waited for the police to come pick him up. His friends surrounded me, threatening to put a contract out on me if I didn't let him go. I ignored them.

To my surprise, some of the bar's other patrons—folks tied to the Youngstown mafia—spread the word that anyone who touched me would face their wrath. They pulled me aside and said, "You treat everyone the same. You've always been fair and respectful, and we respect that. We've got your back."

That night, my decision reinforced the tone I'd set with the regulars. The fights stopped, and a sense of calm took over the club. My role was to keep order, and everyone knew I'd do whatever it took to make that happen. That was the full extent of my purpose back then.

But restlessness crept in. I knew I could do better for myself than being a nightclub bouncer, and I hatched a plan to start a business of my own supplying talent to the three clubs I'd eventually served. I excitedly shared my big idea with a gas station owner, the one normal guy I looked up to in that town.

He wasn't impressed. Glancing from me to the road, he said, "See that guy driving the Cadillac?" I spotted a frowning, overweight man with bags under his eyes, puffing a fat cigar. "Chase that big idea of yours and you'll end up looking like him."

It didn't take a minute for me to realize that was not my path. Nightclubs weren't my calling. Education awaited. Soon after, I packed my bags and headed back to Duke.

PURPOSE IN ACTION

Living with purpose means tuning in to the world, including family, friends, work, and strangers. It's certainly not about bouncing unsavory characters at a nightclub. Defining and living your purpose takes time and effort. As you focus internally on purposeful *being*, your external relationships blossom, and you become more aware and find greater joy in relationships at work, and in neighborhood, church, or other groups.

Since the days of ancient Greece, philosophers have cautioned that chasing momentary pleasures is a shaky foundation for a good life. It's a trap that can blow up in your face. Happiness and pleasure aren't twins. Confuse them and you're hooked on short-lived thrills, booze, drugs, endless smart phone scrolling, and other quick fixes that can sabotage what truly matters for the long haul. Pleasure is fleeting, often tied to sensory experiences, while happiness is longer-lasting, rooted in values and profound fulfillment.

Viktor Frankl, a psychiatrist who endured the unimaginable horrors of the Holocaust, crystallized this in his transformative book, *Man's Search for Meaning*. Pleasure is not the engine, he argued. It is purpose that keeps us moving. Frankl believed that by grappling with suffering—asking why it's there, choosing how to respond—we sharpen our focus on what's essential. Purpose doesn't erase pain, but it gives us a lens to see it, a framework to bear it, and a reason to push forward.

Frankl's focus on purpose over pleasure sets the stage for understanding life's deeper stakes. This perspective aligns with timeless traditions that view our choices as shaping not just the present, but what comes next. From ancient religious traditions to modern mindfulness movements, the refrain is consistent: This life is a proving ground for what comes next. Our choices go beyond the here and now, shaping not just our days but our destiny. Whether you believe in an afterlife or not, the logic holds: Living with intention leaves a mark.

Embarking on the quest to find and live a purposeful life is the boldest, most worthwhile endeavor you can undertake. Values become clearer and more ingrained with every lesson. Discovering purpose demands introspection. It requires peeling back the layers of who you are and the values you proclaim. Next comes a big dose of commitment to stick with it. But the reward? A life that's not just fuller and healthier but electric with meaning. In the next chapter, we'll dig into the nuts and bolts of this process, starting with the cornerstone: defining your values.

2

Finding Your Values and Virtues

THOSE WHO DRIFT THROUGH LIFE reacting to events often find themselves in a haze of uncertainty. For many, these moments pull them along like a kite caught in shifting winds, their paths dictated by whatever gust blows hardest. There's a different way to make this journey, one that hinges on claiming agency over your path. That agency starts with finding your values and virtues—the foundation of uncovering your purpose, which turns a haphazard existence into a deliberate one.

BEDROCK OF PURPOSE

Purpose doesn't drop from the sky. It grows from the ground up, rooted in your values. They're the convictions you'd stand by when the stakes climb higher, the beliefs about what is important you'd hold even if no one applauded you. They're the scaffolding of your identity, the unseen frame that holds you together.

When your choices sync with these principles, you feel a quiet contentment that your life fits your soul. It might be as simple as lending a hand to a struggling neighbor or biting back a harsh word. But what happens when you stray from those principles? Let's say one of your values is telling the truth. Tension is going to creep in if you dodge a tough truth. The tension is a signal that something is off. This is cognitive dissonance, the mind's way of signifying a breach when your actions clash with your inner code.

While values and virtues are often used synonymously since they both refer to principles and ideals many hold dear such as honesty, charity, and other aspirational qualities, values transform into virtues as we embrace and internalize them. We make those values ours. This transformation is not automatic. It requires a sustained commitment to evaluating and refining one's behavior and objectives.

Many major religions espouse values that are similar, draw us closer to our Creator, and when developed, prepare us for a better life in the hereafter. If you want purpose or confirmation of ethical values, don't ignore teachings that have survived for thousands of years. Delve into the teachings of various religions.

I don't want people to turn away from these insights fearing I am going to push religion. That's not my intent. But we are all "religious" in the sense that everyone adheres to a set of beliefs or values, whether they come from divine guidance, self-realization, the teachings of others, life experiences, or societal norms. My purpose is not to push you into some form of organized religion but to help you "organize your religion" and seek truth finding your place comfortably within humanity.

To this end, the lens I have used to explore the values and virtues I cherish most is one used by major religious traditions: love, compassion, humility, meekness, charity, honesty, gratitude, forgiveness, courage, repentance, and service.

LOVE

Love binds all. Love is the heartbeat of human connection. It transcends mere emotion, guiding actions that uplift others, whether through kindness to a stranger, devotion to family, or passion for a cause. Love inspires sacrifice, forgives flaws, and builds bridges across divides.

Love is a fundamental pillar in the framework of human experience, often cited by philosophers, spiritual leaders, and cultural figures as central to a meaningful life. In Christianity, love is famously celebrated as the greatest of all virtues. In 1 Corinthians 13:4-7 (NIV), Apostle Paul describes the enduring nature of love: "Love is patient, love is kind. It does not envy, it does not boast, it is not proud. It does not dishonor others, it is not self-seeking, it is not easily angered, it keeps no record of wrongs. Love does not delight in evil but rejoices with the truth. It always protects, always trusts, always hopes, always perseveres."

Buddhism teaches followers to cultivate an unconditional loving-kindness toward all sentient beings. Hinduism celebrates divine love through narratives of deities such as Krishna and Radha, whose spiritual love affair is a metaphor for the soul's intense love and longing for a personal connection with the divine.

Like the other values and virtues, love is more than a mere emotion. It is active, and it is revered as a vital force in human life, driving individuals and communities toward greater understanding, acceptance, and unity. According to the Dalai Lama, in his book *The Art of Happiness: A Handbook for Living*, it's vital for a lasting world: "Love and compassion are necessities, not luxuries. Without them humanity cannot survive."

COMPASSION

Compassion is universally revered because it extends empathy, kindness, and understanding toward others, particularly during times of suffering. This moral inclination not only promotes emotional bonds between individuals but also fosters a supportive, cooperative community.

Compassionate individuals experience feelings as if they were their own. Empathy transcends mere sympathy. It's sitting on the floor at 2:00 a.m., listening as a friend's voice breaks over a shattered heart, nodding until your eyes burn from exhaustion. It's choosing to carry their burden alongside yours, not out of duty but because their hurt resonates within you.

As Nelson Mandela said, "Our human compassion binds us the one to the other—not in pity or patronizingly, but as human beings who have learnt how to turn our common suffering into hope for the future."

Many religions teach that showing compassion to others is akin to honoring and serving God. Jesus Christ's ministry was marked by acts of compassion: feeding the hungry, healing the sick, and comforting the sorrowful. In Buddhism, compassion involves taking action to alleviate the universal nature of suffering. Muslims are repeatedly encouraged in the Qur'an to emulate divine qualities by showing mercy and compassion to draw the believer closer to God. Compassion in Hinduism is tied to the concepts of dharma (divine law; moral duty) and karma (action and subsequent reaction), while in Judaism compassion or "chesed" is a fundamental attribute of Jewish ethics.

By practicing compassion, religious communities not only follow their sacred teachings but also contribute to a more humane and just world. As does anyone who practices compassion.

HUMILITY

Humility doesn't crave recognition but shines through selfless actions, serving and uplifting others. Those who exemplify humility are quick to forgive and slow to anger, are not judgmental, and feel a genuine joy in the successes of others. The humble person listens intently and patiently, learns eagerly, and grows quietly, always open to the wisdom of others. They remain gracious in triumph and steadfast in setbacks. This value nurtures empathy, kindness, and collaboration, prioritizing connection over competition.

Having humility does not mean you should diminish yourself. In fact, you will likely appreciate and value all life, including your own, more intensely. It is about not putting yourself above others and looking outward, seeing and considering others instead of being self-absorbed.

All religions suggest that humility liberates people, enabling them to gain a higher spiritual awareness. In the New Testament, Philippians 2:3 (NKJV) expresses it well: "Let nothing be done through selfish ambition or conceit, but in lowliness of mind let each esteem others better than himself."

In the teachings of Islam, humility is a sign of strength, not weakness, reflecting the surrender of one's ego to the will of Allah. In Buddhism, it is about acknowledging the limits of one's knowledge and experience, helping individuals break free from the cycles of desire and ego-driven behavior, ushering them toward enlightenment.

MEEKNESS

Meekness is not to be confused with weakness or submissiveness. Far from timidity, it's a deliberate choice to prioritize peace over strife. It's a quiet strength, embodying patience and restraint. Meekness also builds trust, promoting unity through quiet confidence.

Embracing meekness can improve one's relationships through a non-confrontational and understanding demeanor. Socially, it encourages a culture of respect and peace, where conflicts are resolved through dialogue and compromise, not aggression and dominance.

Across religious traditions, meekness is portrayed not as weakness but as a formidable strength marked by self-control, humility, and a disposition toward peace. It challenges the common perception of power, proposing that true influence and lasting legacy come from a gentle, steadfast spirit guided by ethical and spiritual principles.

In Christianity, meekness is frequently emphasized as a virtue that Jesus Christ himself embodied and preached. As one of the Beatitudes in the Sermon on the Mount, Jesus declared, "Blessed *are* the meek: for they shall inherit the earth" (Matthew 5:5, KJV), underscoring the promise of ultimate reward for those who are humble and restrain themselves, despite perhaps having the power to do otherwise.

In Judaism, meekness is often associated with righteousness and moral courage. Moses, one of the greatest prophets and leaders in Jewish history, is described as "very meek, above all the men which *were* upon the face of the earth" (Numbers 12:3, KJV).

CHARITY

Charity is selfless love in action, driven by compassion and generosity. It gives without expecting reward, offering time, resources, and/or kindness for the benefit of others. Rooted in empathy, charity sees need and responds with care, whether through a warm meal, a listening ear, or a helping hand. It reflects a heart open to all, exemplifying the belief that every act of giving enriches both giver and receiver.

Many personal benefits flow from charity. An Ohio State University study, published in *The Journal of Positive Psychology*, showed that acts of kindness lead to greater reductions in depression and anxiety and higher satisfaction with life compared to other interventions.

The New Testament and the parable of the Good Samaritan (Luke 10:23-37) highlight the importance of showing compassion and kindness to others. Christians are encouraged to give to the poor, care for the sick, and assist those who are less fortunate. In Islam, charity requires Muslims to purify their wealth and aid those in need through obligatory alms giving and voluntary charity. The concept of charity is also a central tenet of Judaism, Hinduism, and Sikhism.

HONESTY

Honesty builds a currency stronger than gold. It is a commitment to truth in words and actions, speaking sincerely, even when it's hard, and owning mistakes with courage. It's more than simply telling the truth. It's an active, ongoing pursuit of the truth. It carries with it a tender urgency to listen respectfully to opposing views that challenge our assumptions while avoiding contention that blocks discovery. Honesty builds authentic connections, free of deception, engendering respect and understanding. Beyond avoiding lies, it's living your life with transparency and integrity. Honesty isn't always easy, but it strengthens relationships and grounds us in what's real.

In many religions, honesty is not just about telling the truth but living truthfully in the eyes of the divine, reflecting an alignment between one's inner values and outward actions. In Christianity, honesty is rooted in the Ten Commandments, specifically the directive against bearing false witness.

Similarly, in Islam, honesty is seen as a reflection of one's faith in Allah, and being truthful is considered a reflection of one's inner purity. In the Hadith, the Prophet Muhammad said, "Truthfulness leads to righteousness, and righteousness leads to Paradise. And a man keeps on telling the truth until he becomes a truthful person. Falsehood leads to

Al-Fajur [wickedness, evildoing], and Al-Fajur leads to the [Hell] Fire, and a man may keep on telling lies till he is written before Allah, a liar" (Ṣaḥīḥ al-Bukhārī 6094; Ṣaḥīḥ Muslim 2607).

In Hinduism, the concept of *satya*, the Sanskrit word for "truth," is a fundamental aspect of the dharma influencing actions and thoughts.

Thus, in a religious context, honesty is a cornerstone that not only supports individual integrity but also serves as a foundation for the collective ethical and spiritual well-being of the community.

GRATITUDE

Gratitude is much more than *feeling* thankful. It's *living* it, which fosters joy in the present. It encourages people to acknowledge life's positives, appreciate the gifts and blessings they receive, and cultivate contentment and humility.

It grounds us, builds resilience, and inspires generosity, reminding us that even in hardship, there's something to hold close and celebrate. When the bus runs late, it's marveling at the fact that you've got somewhere to go, not complaining. It's a habit more than a feeling, one you build by appreciating the small gifts of life.

James E. Faust, a prominent leader in The Church of Jesus Christ of Latter-day Saints, spoke often on themes of kindness, forgiveness, and the importance of family values. In an address at the General Conference of the Church in April 1990, he said, "A grateful heart is a beginning of greatness. It is an expression of humility. It is a foundation for the development of such virtues as prayer, faith, courage, contentment, happiness, love, and well-being."

In Islam, gratitude is considered an essential part of a Muslim's faith and a reflection of one's submission to Allah. Buddhism places a high value on gratitude as a means of cultivating a peaceful mind and mitigating suffering. And Hinduism teaches gratitude through rituals and prayers that express thankfulness to the gods for their blessings.

In all these traditions, gratitude is more than just a feeling. It is a practice that involves recognizing the source of blessings, reflecting on them, and responding with acts of worship, kindness, and service.

FORGIVENESS

Forgiveness encourages letting go of one's resentment, which cankers the soul. It's not excusing harm. It's a conscious decision to release yourself from anger and resentment against someone who has or who you perceive as having harmed you. It facilitates wound healing with understanding. Forgiveness restores trust, mending bonds through empathy and humility. And it puts you back in control of your emotions. It takes strength to forgive, acknowledging pain while freeing the heart from its grip.

Forgiveness is a deep-rooted virtue in religion. Colossians 3:13 (RSV) says, "Forbearing one another and, if one has a complaint against another, forgiving each other; as the Lord has forgiven you, so you also must forgive."

Forgiveness encompasses the act of pardoning, letting go of resentments, and reconciling.

Hinduism teaches *kshama*, which encourages people to forgive those who have wronged them, recognizing that doing so is a virtuous act. Similarly, the Qur'an (Surah Al-Anbya, 21:83) describes Allah as "The Most Merciful of the merciful," emphasizing that mercy and forgiveness are divine qualities believers should aim to emulate.

By forgiving, we allow those who have wronged us the opportunity to improve and grow spiritually. Overall, forgiveness is a powerful act that heals and liberates. It is a blessing to both the forgiver and the forgiven, promoting spiritual growth and a more harmonious existence.

COURAGE

Courage is often associated with physical bravery, but moral bravery is just as critical. It may come in the form of speaking out against injustice or simply doing the right thing even when it is difficult. It's defending and promoting your values, standing up for who you are and what you believe in, listening to new ideas without feeling threatened, taking on opposition without personal offense, and staying the course when storms arise. Courage enables individuals to step outside their comfort zone, take risks for the greater good, protect principles that matter, and pursue new opportunities.

Those who exhibit moral courage inspire change and uphold justice, even when facing criticism or adversity.

In Christianity, courage is seen as a divine gift that enables believers to face trials with faith and perseverance. One of the most relevant verses comes from the Old Testament: "Have not I commanded thee? Be strong and of a good courage; be not afraid, neither be thou dismayed: for the LORD thy God *is* with thee whithersoever thou goest (Joshua 1:9, KJV)." Jesus himself exemplified the ultimate courage: facing suffering, rejection, and crucifixion with unwavering faith in God's plan.

The Bible is filled with stories of courageous individuals like David, who faced the giant Goliath. "Then said David to the Philistine, Thou comest to me with a sword, and with a spear, and with a shield: but I come to thee in the name of the LORD of hosts, the God of the armies of Israel, whom thou hast defied (1 Samuel 17:45-47, KJV)."

In Islam, the prophet Muhammad demonstrated immense courage throughout his life by facing persecution, exile, and battle while always trusting in Allah.

REPENTANCE

Much more than moments of regret, repentance is a deliberate, transformative process in which you take full responsibility for errors, actively making restitution and earnestly seeking forgiveness. Repentance demands courage to confront guilt and humility to embrace vulnerability. Reflecting the capacity to recognize one's missteps and the unwavering commitment to personal growth, it is a key to personal progress. When we recognize, admit, and express regret for mistakes, a burden is lifted, and the joy of repentance blesses us with greater strength and resolve.

For Christians of all denominations, repentance is closely tied to the concept of salvation, a heartfelt turning away from sin and toward God. Often accompanied by prayer, confession, and a committed effort to follow Christ's teachings more closely, it is a continual process, reflecting the ongoing nature of human imperfection and the constant need for divine grace.

For Muslims, repentance means a sincere return to Allah with an open heart and regret for past sins. In Judaism, the practice of repentance reaches its zenith during Yom Kippur, but it is also an integral part of daily life involving introspection, prayer, and seeking forgiveness from those harmed by one's actions before seeking God's forgiveness. Hinduism interprets repentance as part of spiritual purification and karma, acknowledging and learning from mistakes and performing specific penances such as fasting, meditation, and the recitation of mantras.

Repentance serves as a bridge to betterment, enabling individuals to turn away from past mistakes and move toward a more ethical and fulfilling life.

SERVICE

Service transcends personal gain, fostering connections that strengthen communities, cultivating a sense of shared humanity, and transforming both giver and receiver.

In a world often driven by individualism and competition, service stands as a counterbalance, reminding us of our interconnectedness. It challenges us to act with intention and consider how our skills, time, and resources can make a difference. By embracing service as a virtue, individuals contribute to a more equitable and compassionate society where the well-being of all is valued.

Jesus Christ emphasized the importance of serving others as a way to serve God. The Biblical parable of the Good Samaritan, for example, teaches that service to others, especially those in need and from different backgrounds, is a form of moral duty that goes beyond cultural and religious boundaries.

In Islam, service is central to the faith's main values, and Muslims are required to give a portion of their wealth to the needy, promoting a spirit of communal support and equality. In Buddhism, the ideal of the Bodhisattva, an enlightened being who forsakes personal nirvana to help others achieve enlightenment, epitomizes the ultimate form of service. And Hinduism emphasizes service as acts of kindness toward those in lower socio-economic circumstances.

In all these traditions, service is not merely an act but a path to spiritual enlightenment, moral integrity, and community solidarity. It reflects a shared understanding that caring for others is a sacred duty and a reflection of one's devotion to God and humanity. Through service, religious adherents find a potent means of expressing their faith and advancing the common good.

Achieving Purpose

Achieving your purpose means becoming someone who lives according to your values. Success isn't what you do but who you become. As we nurture our virtues, we lay the foundation for a life of purpose and fulfillment. Each choice to prioritize others over self, to listen deeply, and to act with integrity strengthens the qualities that define us. This ongoing cultivation prepares us to embrace the pivotal moments that determine our growth, setting the stage for the next chapter in our journey: putting values and virtues into action toward becoming our best selves.

3

Values and Virtues in Action

AS YEARS GO BY, THE significance of life's activities and achievements dim, prompting us not to ask ourselves "What did I accomplish?" but "Who have I become?" and "What relationships do I enjoy?" Our ultimate satisfaction derives from embodying the values we espouse and converting them into virtues.

Just as athletes dedicate substantial time to training and practice to compete effectively, individuals must make a conscious effort to engage with and embody virtuous behaviors regularly. It's a commitment to actively reflect on one's actions and strive to live our values daily, which leads to them becoming second nature.

Athletes often use visualization techniques to enhance their performance, imagining themselves executing perfect form and responding optimally to various challenges during competition. Similarly, we should employ such mental rehearsals for virtuous behavior, visualizing how we might act in different situations and preparing ourselves to recognize and seize key moments during which our virtues could be tested. This mental preparation allows us to react more effectively and ethically in real-life scenarios, strengthening our virtuous qualities over time.

Our goal is to make the ideal more real. Inevitably, we encounter trials and opposition to our values, but by holding to them, they become ingrained in us as virtues. *Never waste a trial.* Only by overcoming trials do we internalize values and hone our character. Ultimately, we each have to decide for ourselves which values we wish to embody.

Perhaps surprisingly, despite widespread conflict—from global warfare to local disputes in politics and even Little League games—the basic human inclination is toward peaceful coexistence. The root of conflicts, including those in trivial settings, is often the dominance of our base emotions or self-centered desires over our higher values. Selfish, corrupt rulers wreak havoc, but individually, we can do the same in our smaller circles of influence. Our commitment to values can quickly fade when selfish perceptions consume our emotions and ambitions.

Values and virtues aren't just nice words on a page or wishful thinking. When enacted, they form the backbone of a consequential life. Which ones resonate with you? Perhaps gratitude when someone acts kindly toward you or courage when you confront a challenge. Perhaps for you, service is shoveling your neighbor's snowy walk before they wake, not for a pat on the back but because it's cold and you've got a shovel.

Which ones need a nudge? Pick two and turn them into a nightly ritual. As you kick off your shoes and wind down, ask yourself where your values showed up in your behavior that day. Maybe you smiled at a cashier and meant it or forgave an offense. It's a way to weave what you believe into who you are. Start there and watch what grows. Mind, body, and spirit all need regular exercise and nourishment for a balanced, healthy life.

Challenges aren't just hurdles, they're proving grounds. Each time you stick to your values under strain, you solidify them. Over weeks, months, and years, these decisions mold you into someone formed not by what happens around you, but by what you hold inside. That's where purpose emerges. It's not racking up titles, chasing accolades, or boosting the balance in your bank account. It's becoming the person you'd admire if you met them—a living echo of the values you've chosen.

Others see this too. When a coworker says you're reliable and considerate after you stayed late to help or when an elderly neighbor calls to thank you for your kindness after you checked on their well-being, they're acknowledging your values in action, not just your hopes. Purpose isn't once-in-a-while heroics. It's a daily practice through your interactions with family, efforts at work, and your presence in the wider world. When you tie your purpose to your values, you gain a compass that doesn't just point north but maps the whole terrain, showing not just where you stand, but where you're headed, one choice at a time.

Claiming your values is the starting line and living them is the long-distance race. It's not enough to scribble love or honesty in a journal as the values you wish to embrace. You need to consider where your values come to life. These behaviors aren't grand gestures but small, consistent acts that are the true heartbeat of your values.

I'm not suggesting you need to suddenly pay attention to how you embody a host of values. Channel your energy into one or two at a time. You will find that by improving in one or two values, you elevate your awareness and behavior for all values.

EXAMPLES OF VALUES IN ACTION

While your list of values may be different than mine, let's explore how values have shown up in my life and how they can be implemented in daily life.

LOVE

Love weaves itself into the fabric of my daily life through intentional acts of care, connection, and sacrifice. It is a core value from which all others (like honesty, integrity, and service) flow. It manifests in a lullaby sung to a newborn, in the quiet moments shared with a spouse, and when I pause my own plans to answer a friend's plea for help. It might be reflected in the selfless act of providing a loan for a grandchild's first car, enabling their dreams while teaching them responsibility. Love is patient encouragement, like cheering a child's small victories or forgiving a partner's oversight.

Love is the greatest gift, not because it demands grand gestures but because it thrives in the ordinary commitment to making consistent, quiet choices to prioritize others' well-being. It's the heartbeat of human connection, building trust, healing wounds, and forging bonds that endure life's challenges.

COMPASSION

My son-in-law, Grant Beckwith, is an outstanding example of living a values driven life. Grant was thriving as a young lawyer when he received a call from Utah offering him the leadership of the faith-based American Heritage School. After prayer and discussions with his insightful wife, Grant decided to leave his DC law firm for the school even though his income would be considerably less. "I love my work here," he said, "but I feel I can contribute and make a greater impact there."

Instead of pursuing income and material possessions, Grant chose the values of compassion and service. When he joined the school in 2005, there were about 350 students K-8. Today, Grant leads an operation that educates more than five thousand K-12 students with a curriculum that includes not only patriotism and history but also an agricultural farm experience, symphony, sports, and real-life learning. Grant, who's also a stake president in the church watching over eleven congregations and four thousand people, lives compassion day in and day out. "It has been a very fulfilling mission and experience," he says with humility.

On a broader scale, as mentioned earlier, our beloved prophet, President Hinckley, urged grace and compassion to overcome a negative reaction when Southern Baptists flooded into Utah for their annual convention. And closer to home, my brother Lew Jr., is committed to compassion (as well as integrity and family). It shone through when he secured loans that kept the company alive.

HUMILITY

The true meaning of humility struck me at a young age when I displayed embarrassing behavior that was far from humble. I was playing in the Blue-Gray Football Classic, the annual college all-star game in

Montgomery, Alabama, on Christmas Day 1968. And after a successful season, I was feeling invincible.

When the game started, I noticed multiple TV cameras, and since I wasn't going to accept NFL offers, this would be my final football game. I wanted to make sure my family, friends, and fans saw me on TV, but linemen typically didn't get a lot of TV coverage. To make sure I could be seen when the ball snapped, instead of hitting low, I stood tall. My opponent plowed his shoulder into my waist and pushed me back fifteen yards. To my dismay, a teammate yelled, "Get Zirkle out of the game. They're blowing him off the line." I was shocked, but my pride and desire to be noticed caused me to abandon my usual stance for a reckless and embarrassing outcome. Where was my humility?

It showed up later at Clare Pendar when I stepped in to head a department while the manager, who many employees found arrogant and unapproachable, was on vacation. I focused on bringing the team together to create a training manual. I did so in a humble manner, probably because I was so junior to those I supervised, but it served me well. By showing respect, valuing their input, and involving them in the process, I empowered them to take ownership of the solution. The collaborative effort not only produced the manual but also turned team members into trainers themselves. My humility proved to be a powerful tool.

MEEKNESS

As discussed, meekness does not equate to submissiveness or weakness. Later in my career, I was nominated for president of the International Business Brokers Association. I stood out among the membership partly because of my size but also because I didn't drink alcohol or listen to off-color jokes during our socials. The presidency was within reach when a member accused me of self-dealing with our technology although, in truth, she was trying to protect and sell her outdated technology.

Colleagues, aware of my values, watched closely as her attacks grew more vicious. "She sees the world differently, and opposing opinions can be healthy for our organization," I said in response to her behavior. Many expected me to retaliate. Some urged me to bury her with equally savage responses. My restrained approach could easily have been regarded as meekness, but it led to an easy election as president. Later, that member and I became friends.

CHARITY

Acts of charity focus on giving to those in need, often addressing immediate individual needs or more widespread community issues such as donating food to a pantry or fundraising for disaster relief. The emphasis is on generosity and alleviating hardship. Of course, sometimes it can be through financial assistance to those facing hardship.

I once noticed a woman at church who looked utterly exhausted. I knew she was having a tough time raising five young children while her husband was unemployed. I slipped an anonymous envelope with five hundred dollars into her mailbox with a note. "This is for you alone to do something special for yourself."

Later, she discovered I was the sender and emailed describing the gift as "a treasure from heaven." She'd treated herself to some personal items and a lunch with friends.

My company would often buy unsold symphony tickets at half-price and give them to employees. The gratitude was profound. One woman from the assembly line wrote, "My daughter and I dressed up and went to the symphony, an experience we couldn't have afforded otherwise. It meant so much to us."

At IndustryPro's Arizona office, we cherish taking time off to pack food baskets. As we hustle to fill bags with essentials, a playful race kicks off. The activity is energizing, but the true reward is seeing the stacks of baskets prepared for families.

HONESTY

When I became an investment banker (a fancy name for business broker), in helping people sell their businesses, I committed to honesty being my guiding principle and vowed to share the truth in all dealings. I'd gone to schools on negotiation that emphasized tactics like bluffing, misleading, and controlling body language: Don't let them see your eyes. Watch how you sit and talk. It felt dishonest.

When clients asked, for example, "Would the seller take ten million dollars?" I faced a dilemma. Honesty might mean admitting the seller would accept, but my role was to secure the best price. I had a fiduciary responsibility to get the most I could for my client, but I also had a responsibility to be honest.

Candid responses rolled off my tongue. "Determine what the business is worth to you and offer your best price. Then we'll compare your offer to others and select the best fit."

Clients recognized my deviation from standard evasive tactics, making me a more effective intermediary, so my honesty often led to better offers and built trust. I usually got a better deal for the owner and not only upheld my values but also benefited my clients and my career.

At IndustryPro, we embed these values in new hires. Every new employee, regardless of their level, meets with IndustryPro's president on their first day with the company. The exclusive purpose of the meeting is to discuss IndustryPro's mission and values. The first value discussed is integrity, with a focus on being honest at all times. The new employee learns that IndustryPro's team prioritizes integrity over revenue every time. We always provide honest advice to business owners and ensure they have successful M&A outcomes. We coach the employees to respond with transparency, even under pressure, using phrases like, "I understand this matters, but this is my best offer," or to business owners, "Yes, we earn commissions, but if you're not ready to go to market, let's wait until you are." Owners appreciate this principled approach, which builds trust, confidence, and respect.

GRATITUDE

Your joy increases if you regularly reflect on the positive aspects of your life. You benefit by cultivating a mindset of gratitude, focusing on what you have, as opposed to what you don't have. Awakening one day to bemoan some mounting problems, I felt prompted to make a list of what I was thankful for, expecting to come up with a dozen items. To my great surprise, I listed over two hundred items, which buoyed my spirits for days.

A Mayo Clinic Health System article validated my personal experience. The report showed that feeling thankful can improve sleep, mood, and immunity and decrease depression, anxiety, chronic pain, and risk of disease. If there was a pill that could accomplish all this, everyone would be taking it.

FORGIVENESS

The ability to seek forgiveness is vital—so much so that in the preface of this book I asked for the forgiveness of anyone who encountered the brash young Fred Zirkle. Forgiveness involves letting go of resentment and choosing compassion, even when we have been wronged. Practicing forgiveness daily, for both significant and minor grievances, transforms how we interact with others. It's not about excusing harm but about freeing ourselves from anger's grip.

Recognize when you've been hurt but avoid dwelling on blame. For example, if a coworker overlooks your contribution in a meeting, note the sting but don't let it fester. Calmly address it or let it go, understanding they may have been distracted. Seek forgiveness proactively. If you've wronged someone, own it. Let's say you forgot a colleague's important event. Tell them you're sorry you missed the presentation and let them know you'd love to hear about it. Then forgive yourself for your forgetfulness. You missed a deadline? Own up to it with those who need to know, make amends, and forgive yourself. Avoid criticizing yourself. Reflect, learn, and move forward.

Of course, these examples pale into insignificance when you consider the words of Charlie Kirk's widow, Erika. Addressing seventy thousand people packed into State Farm Stadium in Glendale, Arizona, and tens of millions online and on television, she extended forgiveness to her husband's assassin. Fighting back tears she said, "On the cross, our savior said, 'Father, forgive them, for they know not what they do.' That man—that young man—I forgive him. I forgive him because it's what Christ did. And it's what Charlie would do."

"The answer to hate is not hate," she added. "The answer—we know from the gospel—is love. Always love. Love for our enemies. Love for those who persecute us."

There can be no greater expression of forgiveness than that given to the murderer of a loved one.

COURAGE

Courage manifests daily in confronting fears and embracing challenges with resolve, not because you're fearless, but because the right action matters. It's raising a trembling hand in a silent meeting to call out an injustice, your voice steady despite your sweaty palms. It's making a tough call—ending a toxic relationship or reporting unethical behavior at work—knowing the fallout may be heavy.

Courage is walking through a dark night, heart racing, to help a stranded neighbor. Courage is striving to master a new skill, like public speaking, despite early failures. It's a parent standing firm on boundaries with a defiant teen. It's a student asking a question in class, risking embarrassment to learn. Courage is admitting a mistake to a colleague, owning it fully. Sometimes it's pursuing a career change despite uncertainty. It's volunteering for a daunting project or defending a stranger from unfair criticism. Courage thrives in these moments, pushing you to act with integrity, grow through discomfort, and choose the hard path when it aligns with what's right.

REPENTANCE

Repentance starts with self-awareness: recognizing a mistake, feeling genuine remorse, and committing to change. Tools like journaling, prayer, or seeking honest feedback from trusted friends can reveal areas for improvement. Without reflecting on one's actions, and then taking corrective measures, growth cannot happen.

The president of my church urges us to experience the joy of repentance on a daily basis. Every day? Why not? I certainly make mistakes every day. If I don't acknowledge, repent, or correct daily, am I improving? I have learned the joy of daily repentance and I confess my sins at church weekly, seek forgiveness, and through atonement's grace, I find renewal and strength to overcome weaknesses.

SERVICE

At its heart, service is an expression of love and humility in which one identifies the needs of others and responds with heartfelt care. This may include volunteering at a soup kitchen, spending time with a lonely neighbor, sharing knowledge to uplift others, or providing resources to ease suffering. The absence of expectation for reward or recognition distinguishes service from transactional interactions, making it a pure and altruistic endeavor.

Once I coordinated community volunteer opportunities for employees and encouraged them to participate during paid work hours, but it was only when I physically joined in these activities myself that I was reminded of the real joy of service. While building a Habitat for Humanity house in Spokane, the camaraderie fashioned an uplifting bond, and we all left with happier hearts.

During this project, my employees discovered I was a real human, and I grew more appreciative of them as individuals. We were all equals constructing this house together. When you do something of service, you always feel good, but doing it as a team is even better. And it was clear to me that personal engagement in service is far more impactful than making remote financial contributions.

After I was let go from Key Tronic and was horribly depressed, my bishop asked me to visit an elderly man in a care home. Despite my initial reluctance, the visit turned out to be a turning point. As I opened the door and looked around, a lady with a strong German accent scooted up to me in her wheelchair. "Well, don't just stand there! Wheel me around!" she said. I laughed and did as instructed. Our conversation brightened my mood.

When I found the man I was asked to visit, initially, he was noncommunicative, but we gradually started talking and played an engaging game of chess. As I left the care home that day, I felt overwhelming gratitude for my health and family, realizing that service had converted my sorrow into thankfulness. The visit uplifted me so much that whenever I felt a bit down, I knew it was time to play chess with my new friend.

On one of my visits to the home, I noticed a woman who always sat motionless, her expression blank, like she was lost in her own world. "I see you here all the time," I said, approaching her. "And I'd love to share a wave with you. I bet you have a beautiful smile. It stings a little when you don't notice me. Could you try waving and smiling next time?"

To my surprise, she turned her head and gave me a warm smile. From that day forward, we'd exchange waves and smiles whenever I walked in, a simple connection that became a source of joy for both of us.

Another meaningful experience came when a hurricane struck Beaufort, South Carolina, about four hours away from my home near Greenville. While a group from my church helped on weekends, weekdays were quiet because most people were at work. I drove down with my chain saw and accompanied by my sister-in-law who lived there roamed the area stopping whenever we saw a fallen tree or someone clearing a damaged yard. "Need a chain saw?" we'd ask.

One day, we spotted a tree leaning precariously on an old trailer. I knocked, and an elderly woman in a wheelchair answered, distressed. She couldn't afford to have the tree removed and feared it would topple and destroy her home. I reassured her I could help. After I carefully removed the tree, she thanked me. "I wish I could repay you, but I have nothing," she admitted.

I smiled. "You can pay me . . . with a great big hug."

She embraced me tightly, tears streaming down her face.

VALUES AS A PATH TO PURPOSE

A strong set of values enhances your awareness and freedom to choose your life's path. Some might argue that adhering to values restricts spontaneity, but it actually illuminates possibilities. Values steer you, helping you work through options to find paths that are in accord with who you are. Without guiding values, distractions easily ensnare you. Without values, every path seems equally valid (or irrelevant), leaving you at the

mercy of circumstance. You might default to the easiest or most immediate option because nothing directs you otherwise.

Values filter out distractions, revealing opportunities that resonate
with your purpose. Living purposefully means reclaiming control by
committing to values and the person you want to be. Trials—moments of
temptation or difficulty—are chances to strengthen your values or falter
by reacting thoughtlessly. Everyone slips occasionally, but a purposeful
life grows from learning to act with intention, using values as a guard rail.

When consistently practiced, values transform into virtues, which
are ingrained habits of character that define who we are. Whatever you
do, do it. We judge ourselves by intent; others judge us by what we do.

Here's how it works:

- **Intention Becomes Action.** A value begins as a belief you hold
  dear. That belief inspires action. For example, if courage is your
  value, you believe it's vital to stand up for what's right, even when
  it's challenging. And you do that.

- **Action Brings Practice.** Values grow into virtues through repeated
  action. When you choose to act courageously, like speaking out
  against injustice or confronting a fear, you establish a pattern.
  Each act reinforces your commitment, making courage feel more
  natural over time.

- **Practice Builds Habit.** With consistent practice, a habit is formed.
  Courage is no longer just an ideal you admire. It's embedded in
  the habitual way you act and respond to life. You act with courage
  instinctively, not to prove a point but because it's woven into your
  being through sustained practice.

- **Habit Becomes Character.** Through sustained habit, courage
  defines you. It's a part of who you are. It shapes how you navigate
  life, becoming a core part of your identity. Your character now
  reflects courage, guiding your decisions and interactions effortlessly.

- **Reflection Deepens Growth.** Pausing to reflect on your actions—
  celebrating wins or learning from mistakes—strengthens the
  value. For instance, if you value repentance, reflecting on errors
  and making amends diminishes remorse while increasing resolve.

Repentance deepens your humility and accountability while cementing it as a lasting virtue.

- **Consider the Context.** Values adapt to the reality of different stages of life. Service as a value might mean volunteering as a young adult, mentoring as a professional, or caregiving as a parent. Each context hones the virtue, making it versatile yet steadfast.

MEASURING PROGRESS

Virtues, then, are values made durable through discipline and intention. This transformation isn't accidental. It requires effort, self-awareness, and commitment to coordinate actions with ideals. Ultimately, virtues are the living proof of our values, shaping not just what we believe but how we show up in the world.

To measure your progress, dig deep and ask yourself probing questions. How do others see you? If you regard yourself as compassionate, would your spouse or business colleagues agree, or would they raise an eyebrow? Picture your legacy. What words would be used to describe you at your funeral? For instance, would they say you were a loving, forgiving person and someone who always helped others?

These questions cut through the fluff, linking your purpose—your reason to get out of bed each day—to the values you hold. They force a reckoning. Are you walking your talk?

It took me a long time to begin to live a purposeful life.

4
Living a Purposeful Life

MY AWAKENING BEGAN IN 1979, at the age of thirty-three. That year I attended education week at Brigham Young University. I had just joined The Church of Jesus Christ of Latter-day Saints and wanted to dig deeper into church doctrine. Among the many voices that week, one that stood out was C. Kay Allen, founder of the Human Values Institute and former speaker of the Utah House of Representatives. He shared his Three Levels of Awareness model, which became a touchstone for my life.

Kay described how we all cycle through these behavioral states, oscillating between destructive impulses and constructive choices. The lowest level (Fear/Anxiety), he explained, is marked by reactivity—anger, fear, or selfishness driving our actions. The middle level (Duty/Justice) reflects a more balanced, functional state, where we meet expectations but rarely exceed them. The highest level (Love/Trust) is aspirational. It's a place of intention, empathy, and alignment with our best selves. What captivated me most were the practical tools he shared to transcend those baser instincts. These tools were self-awareness, emotional regulation, and deliberate action. His words didn't just inspire, they planted a seed of transformation that would take years to fully bloom.

Upon returning home that Sunday, I was buoyant, my mind buzzing with possibility. But by Wednesday I recognized an almost hypocritical jarring dissonance between the ideals I'd embraced and my actions. Eager to bridge this gap, I reached out to Kay and asked if he provided consulting. To my delight, he agreed not only to mentor me personally but also to hold workshops for my company. His involvement illuminated the path toward the man I hoped to become.

Through our sessions, Kay helped me see how emotions can hijack our behavior, pulling us into cycles of regret. His Three Levels of Awareness model became a lens through which I could evaluate my actions. When I snapped in frustration, I was operating from that Fear/Anxiety level, reactive and unmoored. But by pausing to name the emotion and consider my values, I could recognize what level I was operating from and choose a higher plane. The emphasis was not on perfection but on making progress, a slow, intentional shift toward living with purpose. I began to catalog the triggers that threw me off course: stress from deadlines, personal attacks, unmet expectations, even the quiet ache of self-doubt. With Kay's guidance, I learned to meet these moments with curiosity instead of resistance, mentally asking myself some questions: *What can this teach me? How can I respond differently?*

This journey revealed a timeless truth: When emotions overrun our judgment or when we lack the skills to connect with others, a chasm opens between our principles and our practice. Emotions are not our enemy, but they are not our master either. Emotions drive behavior. If unrecognized or unmanaged, they can pull us toward impulsive and even destructive responses. But with awareness and intention, emotions can become signals, not commands. A purposeful life begins by understanding that we *are not* our emotions. We *experience* emotions, but we *choose* our behavior. This is the essence of human freedom.

Life's challenges—temptations, conflicts, hard choices—aren't roadblocks but invitations. They beckon us to embody our values, not succumb to instinct. A heated argument with a loved one might tempt us to lash out, but it also offers us a chance to listen, mend, and further solidify a relationship. We must first define our values with precision to distinguish right from wrong and exercise the moral agency that sets us apart as human beings.

For thousands of years, the world's spiritual traditions have echoed this call to rise above adversity. Beyond religion, fields like psychology and sociology underscore how our choices are shaped by forces like childhood experiences, cultural norms, and peer influences. Yet, amidst these currents, we retain a singular gift: moral agency. Of all God's creatures, Homo sapiens is the only species that enjoys the freedom to make choices based upon moral reasoning. Unlike other animals, whose decisions hinge on survival or conditioning—a dog fetching a ball for a treat, a bird building a nest from instinct—we can choose based on reason, conscience, and vision. A lion doesn't pause to weigh the ethics of its hunt, but we can reflect, adjust, and aspire. Too often, though, we squander this freedom. In moments of anger or fear, we mirror the rest of the animal kingdom, reacting instead of responding.

Our awareness becomes blinded by the emotions controlling our actions. We react, fueled by anger, fear, jealousy, appetite, or even stress. We have all experienced the difference. We feel bad after we fight, attack, or denigrate someone. We feel good when we serve, befriend, or shore up another person. Our own individual growth increases as we strive to act with uplifting values rather than react with negative feelings. This progression shifts our focus from negativity to a better appreciation of other people and their feelings. The big challenge we face after defining our values is to live them, especially when relationships or situations do not go according to plan. True growth emerges when we turn our gaze outward and act in accordance with values like compassion, repentance, and honesty. The test isn't living perfectly but living consistently, holding fast to our principles.

We must remain vigilant, ensuring that our roles—whether in our careers, homes, or communities—don't obscure the underlying purpose that drives us. Purpose isn't a prize to show off or a status to pursue. It's the steady meaning we build into our actions, the pulse of our character. When we ground ourselves in clear values, we create a base for success and recognition in our paths not as goals, but as outcomes of living true to ourselves.

Life will still test us with inevitable challenges, but they need not dictate our course. By clinging to our values, we seize the helm, acting with intention, not drifting at the mercy of circumstance. Picture a boat lost at sea, rudderless and tossed by every wave. Now imagine that same vessel piloted by a steady hand with your values serving as the rudder, cutting through the tide, steering you toward your truest self. The destination isn't a place but a state of being: your best self, formed by a moral compass you've honed over time. The greatest triumph isn't merely enduring tough moments but emerging from them stronger, having held your principles close rather than casting them aside.

The sooner we define our values and pair our lives with them, the richer the rewards we reap. Relationships flourish when grounded in trust and mutual respect, replacing shallow ties with bonds that endure. Confidence blooms where confusion once reigned, freeing us to use our time wisely and sidestep the energy-sapping quarrels that arise from misalignment. Living this way brings real contentment and sharpens our decision-making, cutting through the fog of indecision.

A purposeful life begins with defining values that reflect our beliefs and pursuing them in ways that honor what we stand for. Yet, merely identifying our values is only the first step. The real work lies in breathing life into them. Declaring our intent to live purposefully is a noble spark, but it alone won't light the way to fulfillment. Consider a sport. You might study the playbook and memorize every rule, but mastery comes only when you step onto the field, sweat through the drills, and face the opposition while improving your skills. Life mirrors this. We can recite our values in calm moments, but their strength is forged in the heat of real-world trials.

We need to hold fast to our values so we don't reach the end of our days and look back with regret that we abandoned them. To live with purpose is to embrace this tension between aspiration and action, to see every stumble as a chance to refine our course. It's a commitment to show up, not just for the easy days, but for the ones that are more demanding. Our roles and responsibilities can pull us in a dozen directions, tempting us to measure our worth by our productivity at work or the praise we receive. But purpose doesn't revolve around a paycheck or a pat on the back. It's the quiet certainty that our lives mean something beyond the noise.

My own story took shape through moments of reckoning, none more formative than working alongside my father at the company he founded. It was a crucible that forced me to ask who I am, what I stand for, and what my purpose is. Was I going to mirror myself after his behavior or would I unearth my internal motivation? The interplay of business and family dynamics forced me to consider how these forces impacted us both, for better and for worse.

My father's life, deeply intertwined with his work, taught me dedication and grit, yet it also revealed the cost of a singular focus. It pushed me to sort through what was passed down versus what I truly chose for myself. It's normal for teenagers to rebel against their parents while determining their own values and carving out their own identities. Looking back, I see traces of that rebellion in myself while I figured out my values.

After losing his job at Clare Pendar, my father tried to embrace retirement, but it proved to be a daunting challenge. Most of his energy and time had focused on his work, and without it, he felt lost. "Work is my number one purpose because it allows me to provide for my family," he said, justifying his restlessness. Yet, with a sizable fortune already secured from his executive role at Poly Scientific, financial necessity wasn't the issue. He, like all of us, had a need to feel productive, and productivity usually came from the job.

Unemployment took a toll on him, and his abrupt shift to retirement left a lasting mark on me. It was the first time I'd seen him grapple with depression. His struggle to step away from work and his identity as Mr. Keyboard showed me that success and strong values aren't enough. You need a purpose that goes beyond "building things," even if that purpose once included creating a company and supporting others.

I imagine he must have paused to reflect, asking himself what truly mattered to him and what gave his life meaning. Perhaps he was already

living by lofty principles but hadn't stopped to appreciate his own journey. If he'd taken stock of his achievements, which benefitted many, I
think he could have found more joy. But he fixated on what he lacked
without a job when he might have taken pride in the person he'd grown
into and the meaningful life he was still shaping.

For most of his life, Dad thrived on action and productivity. He loved
tangible outcomes, whether from building businesses or mastering skills
like electrical work, plumbing, carpentry, and masonry—skills he used
to construct two homes. Occasionally, he'd humor Mom with a round
of golf, a boat ride, or a walk, but leisure often left him restless and
downcast. Work (building something) made him feel whole.

Mom saw this clearly. When his first stab at retirement fizzled, she
put her foot down. "The yard's immaculate and the house has been
repainted twice. You've got to get out and do something. There's only
so many times you can prune the trees or touch up the walls. Go find a
job." That ultimatum stimulated the creation of Key Tronic.

In my case, I'd become more aware of the need to visualize and live
my values after my return to Duke from West Virginia, but I was still
primarily focused on *doing* things rather than on *being* the person I wanted
to become. I committed to achieving two goals: becoming so dominant
on the football field that a coach would have to put me in the lineup and
jumping from a 2.4 GPA to the dean's list. I did it! The alumni association
even created an award for me: Most Inspirational Player.

Upon graduation from Duke, four doors swung open for me as I
began to seek my life's purpose: join the NFL team, the New York Jets
after they drafted me, accept a job offer on Wall Street, study at Wharton
Business School, or build Key Tronic with Dad. I chose the fourth door.
Dad hired me because he'd seen I was effective at working with people,
respected others, listened to what others had to say, and problem solved
collaboratively. Later that changed. Hundred-hour weeks at Key Tronic
eroded my patience, and I turned into a sharp-edged and intimidating boss.

Working for my father complicated my quest to live my values. His
management style did not fit me. Dad's admirable values—such as honesty,

courage, and loyalty—shined bright, and while I admired and respected him, I knew it was critical to be my own person and blaze my own trail.

A defining moment came one payroll day at Key Tronic when our banker froze our account without notice after we'd issued employee paychecks. I was the only officer with any savings, so I gave employees cash draws to get through the weekend. Those good people came into my office, one by one, apologizing for needing thirty or forty dollars to cover food, gas, or other essentials. I'd reply, "Goodness, please don't apologize for asking for a small part of your earned paycheck."

This was a huge trial for me, the company, and them. I had limited savings and could only write small checks. Yet common values of compassion and honesty carried us through until my brother, Lew Jr., loaned us money. More notably, this financial disaster uncovered our values and respect for each other—employer, employees, and family members. It brought us all closer, and my commitment to honor people grew.

At the age of fifty-six, my father sought life insurance to secure a business loan only to face immediate rejection. The insurers informed him that a comprehensive review of his health determined he was uninsurable. Worse still, he was told they estimated his life expectancy to be no more than five years. Along with gout, he was grappling with heart irregularities. Shaken, Dad summoned me to his office and confessed that the news left him too rattled to bear additional stress. Caught off guard, I resorted to humor to mask my unease. "Well, Dad, maybe this will finally convince you to take it easy."

But the moment I stepped out of his office, I dialed the member of the immediate family who was a doctor, Lew Jr. He didn't hesitate to step in and take charge of Dad's medical care. Beyond that, Lew Jr. tackled the company's dire financial straits, scrambling to borrow and scrape together every dollar he could to keep operations afloat.

Lew Jr.'s efforts pulled Key Tronic back from the brink of collapse. Ignoring the wary counsel of financial advisors, Lew Jr. secured loans that kept the company alive. His commitment to compassion, integrity, and family values was the solid base of that survival. Without it, the company would have crumbled.

Gradually, the personal computer boom fueled a surge in orders, cash flow turned positive, and managers rose to the occasion. Astonishingly, Dad's health took a turn for the better as well. It's often said that success, whether in business or personal life, can bolster your well-being, and Dad's recovery seemed to prove it.

Lew Jr.'s values of loyalty and compassion not only saved the company but also reflected a deeper truth about personal growth and purpose. His story reminds us that true transformation rarely happens in isolation. Becoming your best self is not a do-it-yourself project. It demands that we tune in to our conscience, that still, small voice nudging us toward light. Living without this light is akin to grass shielded from the sun. The grass may survive but only in a weak, unnourished condition, far below its potential. If we commit to live by righteous values, even if it is late in life, we must not fret about time lost. What matters is who we have become and our personal growth.

I've made the analogy of values being the rudder that steers you toward your destination, but even the best of sailors can become disoriented in rough seas and stormy weather. Even so, that still, small voice of the spirit or conscience is like the beacon from a distant lighthouse offering direction and guidance. Every human being is born with an innate spiritual or moral self. For some, the recognition of spiritual or moral promptings may come gradually through a process of self-discovery, contemplation, or transformative life experiences. For a few, it may strike like a lightning bolt, even if the impulse that led to the sudden epiphany had been building, unrealized, for many years. However it occurs, this journey of spiritual or moral awakening yields meaning, purpose, and connection beyond the material realm.

The ego self often seeks to overcome the spiritual/moral self, tossing us from one gratification or battle to another. We can choose between calmly listening or angrily attacking or between feelings of jealousy and anger versus feelings of love and calmness. Which voice we listen to is our choice.

We're born with a conscience, which as children is an inner voice that tells us things like, "Don't hit your brother or sister," or "Give Mom a hug." By continually listening and acting on moral promptings, conscience grows into a steady moral companion. If we sincerely listen, we receive jewels of truth, hope, and encouragement. The opposing negative voice of the ego self never gives up. It repeats itself with all sorts of rebuttals. For example, when prompted to check on a sick neighbor, the voice within us that is self-absorbed says, "Don't bother her. She's probably sleeping. You have too many other things to do. Last time she didn't even thank you. Check on her later. Someone else will probably check on her anyway."

So how do we strengthen our connection to our spiritual or conscience-driven self? First, we humbly acknowledge the need for guidance and instruction. We cannot live a fully purposeful life going solo. Next, we nurture the spirit or voice of the conscience through meditation, mindfulness, or prayer. And most important, we act on our highest internal promptings, which come from spirit or conscience.

Whether it's in business, personal relationships, or community engagement, values sustain and define us. They form the bedrock of a life lived with purpose, guiding us toward not only achieving our goals but also building an inner, peaceful confidence. When we live our values, we align ourselves with something bigger than our individual selves.

Some seeds never sprout. Drought, poor soil, or harsh conditions can keep them dormant, unable to break through to grow. Similarly, when you let stress or emotional tension build, you stagnate, unable to evolve into your fuller self. But your spirit—your inner voice, whether you call it soul, spirit, or conscience—can guide you to new growth. Like a seed breaking through the earth, you'll emerge ready for what's ahead. No more inward, self-focused thinking! Defining and living by your values can nurture meaningful relationships, boost confidence, and bring contentment. If you have not defined your values or have defined them but are not consistently living them, doing so will be akin to rebirth for you. And a vibrant new world awaits that rebirth.

For those standing on the cusp of this rebirth, the path forward begins with understanding yourself anew. And for those who have already defined their values and are doing their best to live them, the path forward is enriched by enhanced self-understanding. The Three Levels of Awareness model, described in the next chapter, offers a framework for this journey, helping you navigate your emotions and behaviors with clarity. By embracing this tool, you can spur your inner voice into purposeful action, setting the stage for a life of joyful fulfillment and growth.

5

Three Levels of Awareness

WHEN YOU HAVE A CLEAR vision of the person you want to become, your next step is to adjust your behavior to match that vision. The Three Levels of Awareness model (created by C. Kay Allen, as mentioned earlier) is a powerful tool in this process that allows you to identify and understand your emotions effectively, categorizing them into distinct behavior levels. This is crucial because it helps you see your emotions not as obstacles but as signals guiding your actions. It guides you to gain insight into yourself, empowering you to handle challenges with confidence.

The model also highlights key moments when you can use your emotions to your advantage. A key moment is a trigger, usually stemming from a trial or confrontation. Triggers can take us into negative spirals, but if you catch yourself being triggered, you can harness the emotions in ways that propel you toward your goals. By recognizing these key moments, you can alter potential setbacks into catalysts for personal growth and development, an approach that not only develops resilience but also enables you to make consistent progress toward becoming the person you aspire to be.

The three levels, outlined in Allen's book, *Journey from Fear to Love: 6 Concepts and 6 Skills that Will Change Your Life*, are:

- Fear/Anxiety
- Duty/Justice
- Love/Trust

We all cycle through all three phases over time—and sometimes even within a matter of hours. Our aim is to catch ourselves when key moments erupt so we can bring our values to bear instead of letting emotions fuel destructive behavior.

FEAR/ANXIETY

Fear/Anxiety is the lowest emotional state, and living here can be exhausting, lonely, and overwhelming. We've all been here but, hopefully, not for long. People stuck in this mindset often feel they're constantly fighting an uphill battle with little control over their lives. Their self-esteem is low, and they tend to believe that external forces—whether people, circumstances, or even luck—are in control of their fate. Because of this, they struggle to make confident choices or take ownership of their lives. They put up emotional walls to protect themselves and often rely on either aggressive behavior or quick retreats to hide their insecurities.

To them, life isn't about growth, joy, or purpose. It's about survival. Every day seems like a new fight to stay afloat, and they often have an "I'll get you before you get me" mindset. They see others not as allies or friends but as competition, threats, or obstacles to overcome. This dog-eat-dog perspective makes it difficult to form genuine connections because trust is in short supply. Much of their energy goes into defending themselves, tearing others down, or worrying about what might go wrong. Instead of focusing on personal growth or meaningful goals, they operate from a place of fear, constantly looking over their shoulder, bracing for the worst, or second-guessing every decision.

Because fear is at the root of everything they do, they tend to struggle with self-respect and respect for others. When they're in an aggressive state, they become greatly suspicious and need to dominate and control the people around them. They may try to manipulate situations, impose their will, or keep others at arm's length because they simply don't trust anyone. On the other hand, when they're in a passive state, they give up control entirely, preferring to let others take the lead, even if it means sacrificing their own happiness or well-being. They might find themselves in toxic relationships, working at jobs they hate, or simply aimlessly drifting through life because they believe they have no say in how things turn out. They think fight or flight are the only options, but taking control of their lives actually means facing issues and taking constructive action.

When faced with problems, their instinctive response isn't to face them head-on but to flee, fight, or surrender. This tendency can make minor setbacks feel like massive failures, reinforcing their belief that life is unfair and out of their hands. Over time, this mindset takes a serious toll, not just emotionally but physically as well. Anxiety-related health problems, chronic stress, and even depression often go hand in hand with this way of thinking and behaving.

What's even more difficult is that some people stuck in this state don't realize they have the power to change. Maybe they were never shown another way, or they've been surrounded by negativity for so long they don't believe a better life is possible for them. They remain locked in this cycle of anger/fear, convinced the world is harsh and unforgiving, a place where only the strongest, luckiest, or most ruthless survive.

The truth is, this mindset doesn't need to be permanent, and it's not the only way to live. But until they realize they have the ability to step out of it, fear and anxiety will continue to hold them back from the happiness, connection, and the fulfillment they deserve.

DUTY/JUSTICE

The Duty/Justice level is a huge step up from living in constant fear and anxiety, and for good reason. It's reflective of a life that feels structured, fair, and secure. People at this stage are guided by a strong feeling of responsibility, honor, and justice, and they take their obligations seriously. They're usually the kind of people you can count on. They show up, do their job, and make sure they hold up their end of the bargain.

But beware. If a Duty/Justice individual is threatened, they may put their values aside and jump into battle. We observe this when usually good individuals going through divorce seek to destroy their ex.

A person at this level generally "does their part" but rarely more than what's expected. They're dependable and honest, and they care a lot about how they are perceived by others. Status matters, and so does reputation. This means they follow the rules, not necessarily because they believe in them but because they feel they *ought* to. They don't want to be seen as irresponsible, lazy, or immoral.

For example, someone at this level might think they need to drive at fifty-five miles an hour because they don't want a ticket without considering that they should drive safely because it protects others. This person is nice to their neighbors as long as the neighbors are nice to them. They like the HOA as long as the HOA doesn't fine them. Their actions are largely shaped by external consequences and societal expectations, not innate moral convictions.

In many ways, this lifestyle is far more comfortable than living in fear. It offers predictability, stability, and control. People at this stage often discover fulfillment in being good workers, responsible parents, and contributing members of society. Life, at least on the surface, seems satisfying. But here's the catch: It can also be a trap.

Since this way of living provides structure and security, many people settle into a permanent rut without ever questioning whether there's something more. Life becomes a routine, a checklist of responsibilities rather than an experience of joy or connection. Relationships tend to be practical rather than genuinely warm and intimate because emotional bonds may seem unnecessary or even unrealistic.

Someone at this level might view love and connection as secondary to obligation. They may think that being a good spouse means providing for their family rather than creating love, joy, and emotional closeness. They focus on what they're *supposed* to do and not what they truly feel.

Many people spend their entire lives in this phase, content with its relative comfort. But for those who crave a more fulfilling existence, it's just another steppingstone. The real challenge is recognizing life doesn't have to be just about duty and justice. It can also be about passion, meaning, and authentic connection. Would you rather live a safe, structured life or take the leap toward something richer and more meaningful, like the Love/Trust level?

LOVE/TRUST

At the highest level of personal growth and fulfillment, Love/Trust is a way of living that goes beyond duty or fear and into something truly life altering. This is the level where life becomes richer, more satisfying, and ultimately, more successful. It's here that a person stops simply *doing* and starts *being*—loving, open, and trusting.

A person at this level doesn't act out of obligation or fear. They don't do things because they *ought* to or because they're afraid *not* to. Their choices come from a more authentic place: I *want* to. What makes this possible? Self-esteem, self-awareness, and a broader understanding of life.

Someone at the Love/Trust level doesn't rely on external validation to feel worthy. Their confidence isn't built on status, approval, or success. Feeling of value comes from an intrinsic sense of self-worth and even divine connection. Love/Trust individuals don't need to control or manipulate situations for security. They're willing to take risks, especially when it comes to relationships.

This openness allows them to build significant connections with others. They don't hold back out of fear of rejection. They aren't afraid to be vulnerable, to share their true thoughts and feelings, or to accept love without suspicion. They understand that trust is not just given, it's built through honesty, consistency, and mutual respect. They find real meaning in serving and in helping others lay down personal selfish desires for a higher, more rewarding relationship with a power bigger than themselves. They lay aside the ego self and align with a higher power, putting their faith, for instance, in a perfect being like Jesus Christ.

Someone living at Love/Trust level doesn't try to dominate life, they govern themselves as they relate to it. They recognize that while they may not control everything that happens, they do control their responses. This awareness allows them to embrace both their strengths and limitations without insecurity. Instead of pretending to be perfect or hiding their flaws, they're comfortable acknowledging them. As far as they're concerned, mistakes are not failures. They just give us more opportunities to grow.

Similarly, they extend this acceptance to others. This doesn't mean they agree with everyone or approve of every action, but they see people for who they truly are—flaws and all—without judgment. They act with integrity, led by an inner moral compass that values what is right and mutually beneficial as opposed to what is merely convenient or socially expected.

At the most profound levels of Love/Trust, relationships become partnerships in growth. An equal relationship, whether in marriage or a long-term commitment, is seen as an adventure, not as just a contract. It's much more than companionship or duty. It's an intense, exhilarating connection.

In such a relationship, unconditional acceptance creates a safe space for both partners to be their truest selves. There is no need for pretense or control. Instead, both are free to share their most intimate thoughts, concerns, dreams, and desires without fear of judgment. They inspire each other, challenge each other, and bring out the best in each another. Living at the level of Love/Trust goes beyond personal happiness to the creation of a world of greater meaning, stronger relationships, and genuine fulfillment. And for those who reach this level, life is truly extraordinary.

MOVING UP AND DOWN THE LADDER

No matter where you are on this spectrum of personal growth, you are not stuck there. The anxious, fearful person doesn't have to stay trapped in self-doubt forever. The person living by duty and justice doesn't have to miss out on fulfilling experiences. Even those who operate from a level of love and trust can continue to expand, refining their awareness and moving into even greater possibilities.

As we move from one level to another, new insights shift how we see ourselves, how we think, and ultimately, how we behave. The real question isn't "Can we change?" We can. The real question is "What can we do to make life, relationships, and ourselves better?"

There are no sharp boundaries between these levels. It's a continuum, not a set of locked doors. And this is not a linear pathway moving in one direction. There is both forward and backward movement. We develop awareness and grow, but we're human. We also slip and stumble. The process of breaking free from Fear/Anxiety isn't about flipping a switch. It's about learning and unlearning, about shedding old patterns and embracing new ones.

The first step to moving beyond Fear/Anxiety is to recognize that this state of mind is like being trapped in a cycle of failure and limitation. To break out, we must develop a few critical abilities.

- Authenticity and integrity: The ability to be real, drop pretenses, let go of manipulation, and act in alignment with our true thoughts and feelings.
- Self-Control: Instead of being ruled by fear or impulse, we develop inner stability.
- Mutual growth in relationships: We shift from win-lose thinking to win-win, seeking relationships that are equal and reciprocal.

What are the abilities needed to break out of Duty/Justice?
- Harnessing harmful behavior: Confront and ask for common agreement.
- Listening, not blaming: Being honest but not accusatory. It's important to place responsibility properly.
- Not trying to get even: There's no place for revenge.

As we embrace these principles, we stop playing social games and show up genuinely, as ourselves. When stressed, we ask ourselves if we're making things better or worse. Reaching Love/Trust involves learning new skills and becoming the embodiment of those skills. At this level, you're no longer just someone who *practices* love, honesty, and trust, you *are* love, honesty, and trust.

Here, life takes on new depth. You don't just react to the world, you integrate everything—your mind, emotions, body, and spirit—into a harmonious whole. You begin to see possibilities where others see obstacles. As C. Kay Allen put it, "It is at Love/Trust where the flowering of the human experience occurs. The price paid to be here is high, but the rewards are great." Why is the price high? Because it requires courage. These rewards require vulnerability and the willingness to step beyond ego, status, and what society tells us we *should* do. We look inward, heal, and extend that healing outward.

Those who taste Love/Trust see the world with a clearer vision. They understand the Fear/Anxiety world is, as C. Kay Allen wrote, "a miserable, hostile, self-defeating jungle where people learn to fail and indeed teach others to fail." It's not because they're bad people but because they haven't yet learned the principles that lead to true mental and emotional health. Similarly, Love/Trust individuals understand that those living in the Duty/Justice world, while far better off than those in Fear/Anxiety, still haven't fully unlocked their potential. They live responsibly but not freely.

But here's the key point: Love/Trust individuals don't look down on others. They see the potential in everyone. They see a giant within each person, a version of them that is capable of more, worthy of more, and ready for more. They don't put others down, they lift them up. And they're willing to help others find that version of themselves. Not by force, not by judgment, but through patience, understanding, and belief. They know that when one person grows, everyone benefits. Reaching Love/Trust isn't the end of the road but the beginning of something even greater. Those at this level continue to expand their awareness, their depth of love, and their ability to inspire and uplift others. The journey never truly ends. It just keeps cycling upward into greater connection, wisdom, and fulfillment as they let that inner spirit be their guide.

We all cycle up and down through each of these stages. The cycle can consume years or minutes. The key to purposeful behavior lies in recognizing our feelings which, in turn, identify what level of awareness we're at and its corresponding behaviors. Often, emotions instantly flare up, and before we know it, the reactive damage is done. We need an internal alarm that says, "Alert. Key moment. Stay in control of your emotions. Don't say or do something that makes matters worse and something you will regret."

THE THREE LEVELS CHECKLIST

The following chart provides a good checklist of the three levels. Take time to study and understand all the elements. Be prepared to return again and again to make sure they are ingrained in your mind and behavior. Doing so can help assure a more consequential and enjoyable life.

FEAR/ANXIETY

"I'll get you before you get me." The focus is on *getting*.

Emotions & Perceptions	Characteristics & Values	Awareness
Angry, fearful.	Anger and fear fuels reactions.	Sees people as threats or personal gain. Not value driven. Ignores others' views and feelings to win.
Anxious, insecure, and defensive.	Puts up walls/barriers. Attacks or flees rather than seeking to understand. Projects a false facade.	False pride. Loses self-control. Fear of failure. Manipulative. Seeks recognition. Life is a jungle. Trusts no one.
Jealous, self-centered.	"What's in this for me?" Attitude of "us against them." Seeks immediate gratification.	Compares self against others. Wants more. Focus on self restricts seeing the bigger, grander world.
Feels like the victim. Not happy.	Blames others. Sorry for self. Tries to impose his own reality.	Does not take responsibility (victim mentality). Falls into a small self-centered world. Reacts rather than taking control of self.

DUTY/JUSTICE

A conditionally satisfied state. Keeps score: "I'll treat you as you treat me." The focus is on *doing*. Solving problems becomes more important than people.

Emotions & Perceptions	Characteristics & Values	Awareness
Satisfied with self.	Conforming. Comfortable while self-improvement is not a priority.	Labels people (political party, neighborhoods, socio-economic level) as "good" or "bad." Seeks security.
Expects others to follow the "rules."	Submits to rules. "I'll be nice to you if you'll be nice to me." People are good if they like me. Gets even if offended.	Loyal to close circle of friends. Seeks to get even if trespassed against. Holds a grudge. Cuts off "offender" rather than forgiving.
Self-image can override values. Ego based.	Must be better than others. Seeks approval and security. If offended, may set values aside to fight and defend.	Performs duties. Perceived world comprised of family and group (bowling team, club, or circle of friends). Others are Okay if they're like me.

LOVE/TRUST

This is the happy, motivated state. The focus is on *being*. Serving others becomes paramount.

Emotions & Perceptions	Characteristics & Values	Awareness
Happy and grateful for faith, family, friends, nature, and opportunities.	Guided by moral compass, love for others, and a higher power. Seeks win/win with others.	Believes in a cause bigger than self. Eager to share joy, understanding, and purpose with others.

Peaceful while striving to improve. Confident in self. Perceives the importance of values. Strong yet humble.	Dedicated to honesty and truth. Makes choices consciously. Places values above self-interest.	Open to others' ideas and perceptions. Aware of and considerate of all without compromising values.
Respects, loves, and strives to enhance others. Compassionate.	Does not blame. Quick to forgive. Admits own mistakes. Pleased with others' successes. Listens to and encourages others. Accepts imperfection in self and others.	Sees a much bigger world than self. Not focused inward but outward. More a servant than a recipient.
Confident in self and path taken.	Not easily offended. Generous and giving. Slow to anger. Quick to forgive.	Eager to share joy, understanding, and purpose with others. Acknowledges a higher power that provides and guides.
Attuned to spiritual promptings.	Reflects, mindfully evaluates, and listens while seeking to improve through greater awareness.	Views a world much bigger than self that includes others and their feelings. Finds pleasure in supporting others and their aspirations.

BEHAVIOR TIED TO VALUES

The Three Levels of Awareness model is a powerful framework designed to help you take control of your life rather than being whiplashed by the whims of your emotions or the unpredictability of various situations. This model is more than just a psychological tool. It serves as a strategic template for intentional living, helping you to embody the person you strive to be. It promotes an enlightened form of behavior that enhances your interactions with others, furthering environments rich in love and trust.

At its essence, the model is a blueprint that ties your behavior to your values. It encourages you to adopt behaviors that not only uplift *you* but also benefit those around you. As C. Kay Allen often reminded me,

"Our purpose is to make the ideal more real and the real more ideal." By employing this model, you gain a vital mechanism for self-regulation, enabling you to recognize when you deviate from your ideal path and then course correct.

The goal is to rise through the three levels, ideally reaching and spending the majority of your time in the Love/Trust tier, where interactions are governed by positive emotions and constructive engagements. However, the reality of life means we often cycle through all three levels. But we constantly strive to accept responsibility for our lives. For instance, when confronted with rising anger—a Fear/Anxiety emotion—the model helps you identify this as a trigger that could foment destructive behaviors if not managed properly and take responsibility for defusing that emotion.

The model emphasizes the development of skills that strengthen relationships instead of eroding them. By encouraging good communication, it challenges you to ask yourself if you're making the situation better or worse in moments of high emotion. Often, this introspection spawns a moment of humility and apology, resetting the interaction to one that is cooperative and geared toward mutual understanding within the Love/Trust mode.

The Duty/Justice level can be somewhat passive, characterized by adherence to rules and rigid labeling of people and situations, which can stifle growth and hinder the potential to help others reach their full potential. Duty/Justice individuals believe in and abide by lofty values, but if someone offends them, the sword replaces values. The model advises against falling into this passive engagement, where people are judged more by the roles they are assigned than as individuals.

Moving to a higher level involves shifting from blame to responsibility. At the Fear/Anxiety and Duty/Justice levels, it's common to attribute one's negative feelings or actions to external factors. The model teaches us to take control by recognizing emotions like jealousy or hurt and choosing forgiveness over resentment. Accepting responsibility means not only acknowledging our shortcomings but also actively seeking solutions.

Reaching the highest state of awareness, Love/Trust, switches our focus from self-centered concerns to the well-being of others. This level is marked by an elevated concern for others, inspired by moral and spiritual insights that enrich our lives and those of others. By taking responsibility for our actions and emotions, we gain mastery over our life's trajectory, making it easier to focus on our goals. This empowered mindset helps us avoid getting caught up in petty disputes or distractions. Controlling emotions like fear and anxiety and squelching the tendency to label frees us from prejudice and helps channel positive energies.

Like most people, my awareness and behavior move through all three levels, but I strive to primarily reside in Love/Trust.

That wasn't always the case. At Key Tronic during our start-up years, I worked around a hundred hours a week and became known for my aggressive management style while our workforce grew rapidly from six initial employees to fourteen hundred employees. Later, as I reflected on both my football days and my early years at Key Tronic, I realized I suffered from what I termed the "uniform perception problem," meaning I failed to see the person behind the uniform. On the football field, my focus had been solely on sidelining whoever was in the way of the next big play. In the business setting, this translated into solving problems while forgetting people, which skewed my management approach.

I overlooked a vital principle of leadership: properly placing responsibility. It is a key strategy in focusing individuals' actions toward positive outcomes. I tended to view my team members as bearers of problems instead of being part of the solution, positioning myself as the sole problem solver. Ideally, I should have engaged more by asking questions, exploring consequences, and encouraging my associates to develop their own problem-solving skills. But my overwhelming schedule often led me to skip these crucial interactions. I found myself blaming or resenting employees for problems beyond their control, becoming a demanding and obstinate leader. If I had leveraged my people skills more effectively, I could have been a far more productive manager. At that time, I mostly operated at the level of Duty/Justice, occasionally slipping into Fear/Anxiety.

My introspective moments on my ranch during which I questioned how I should live my life, led me to commit to a set of values that defined my life's purpose. This journey mirrored learning to snowboard: Initially, my dreams of gracefully carving a path through the snow were met with frequent falls. With time, I found my rhythm, tackling dips, moguls, and deep powder with growing skill and joy. C. Kay Allen's Three Levels of Awareness model gave me tools to address challenges and enhance outcomes for everyone involved at work and in my personal life. This heightened awareness deepened my spiritual connection, clarified my values, and revealed a broader world of people and their possibilities.

Self-Esteem

Self-esteem is a critical aspect of our psychological makeup and is clearly reflected in how we behave. The way we value ourselves influences our interactions with others and our perception of them. For instance, at the Fear/Anxiety level of self-awareness, individuals often struggle with feelings of low self-worth, which leads them to believe others are similarly undervalued, creating a cycle of mistrust and insecurity.

At the Duty/Justice level, people view themselves as fair, honorable, and decent. This self-perception typically extends to others, creating interactions that are based on respect and fairness. However, Duty/Justice individuals are not valiant under stress because they set aside their professed values to "fix" wrongs.

The transformation at the Love/Trust level introduces a significant shift in self-esteem. Here, individuals recognize their own infinite worth and extend that recognition to others. This sense of value transcends mere transactions of fairness or duty. It nurtures a genuine appreciation and respect for the sanctity of all life. When individuals live at this level, they are fully aware of the lower levels of Fear/Anxiety and Duty/Justice but choose to rise above them, embracing a life led by love and trust.

However, reaching this state of Love/Trust is often hindered by the challenges of a Fear/Anxiety-dominated environment. The pressures and struggles of daily life can make it difficult to maintain this elevated perspective, especially when short-term rewards and the need to please others lead to incongruent living. This misalignment can cause individuals to live lives that feel out of focus. They wear masks to meet external expectations instead of acting from their true selves.

Achieving and maintaining a Love/Trust level of self-esteem requires not only recognizing the transient allure of short-term gains but also committing to the more challenging path of long-term self-fulfillment and integrity. When we risk being pulled under by any one of life's many riptides, our values become a lifeline. Being at this level involves a conscious decision to live authentically, valuing oneself and others not just for what we *do* but for the essence of who we *are*. This journey toward higher self-esteem is transformative, enabling individuals to become models of this enriching and fulfilling state of being.

As our self-esteem evolves from superficial validation to a foundation built on love and trust, it naturally paves the way for a serious exploration of emotional intelligence, which serves as a vital bridge between understanding ourselves and effectively interacting with the world. As we cultivate stronger self-worth rooted in love and trust, we become better equipped to tune in to our emotions and those of others, setting the stage for the development of emotional intelligence.

EMOTIONAL INTELLIGENCE

Emotional intelligence is a crucial component of navigating the Three Levels of Awareness model. Our emotions are integral to shaping our behaviors, and as we grow, we often learn to control emotional outbursts. But when emotions are suppressed, they can become even more damaging than they are when they're not suppressed.

Psychologists advocate for getting in touch with our feelings as a way to generate emotional self-awareness and develop emotional intelligence. This involves understanding our emotions and leveraging that insight to manage them and interact meaningfully with others. People with high emotional intelligence are adept at handling a range of emotional situations. Recognizing both negative and positive feelings is the first step. With this awareness, you can enhance positive emotions and mitigate or manage negative ones that skew your perceptions and reactions. Taking a broader perspective offers a clear, realistic view and provides an exciting opportunity to improve ourselves and the world around us.

In my journey toward a more purposeful life, I've discovered that we each carry a personal bandwidth for certain emotions like trust, joy, anxiety, fear, and sadness. Much like our tolerance for noise or temperature, our emotional bandwidth sets a kind of internal range—a ceiling and a floor for how much we allow ourselves to feel.

A personal moment made this vividly clear to me. After leaving my role at Key Tronic, I was driving to my new office when I felt the familiar pressure of anxiety start to build, so I coached myself gently. *Okay, you're feeling anxious. Let's just prioritize. Focus on what really needs to be done today.*

To my surprise, the only truly "critical" task on my list was dropping off a few shirts at the dry cleaners. That was it. And in that realization, the anxiety vanished. That moment revealed something powerful: Emotions, and their impact, don't always arise from external urgency. Sometimes we simply have a set range we operate within, an emotional homeostasis we maintain even when circumstances don't warrant it.

This insight became a turning point. I realized that if I could recognize my preset bandwidths—my thresholds for anxiety, my limits for patience, my capacity for compassion—I could begin to *reset* them. I could reduce the volume on negativity and widen the range for love, joy, and peace.

The first step is awareness. You can't manage what you don't notice. Once we start observing our pattern—like the emotions that trigger stress or how often we withhold compassion even in minor conflicts—we gain the ability to choose differently. We can reprogram our emotional operating system, expanding the bandwidth for the emotions we want to amplify and trimming the range of those we want to abridge.

Living a purposeful life doesn't mean eliminating trials. It means cultivating the capacity to channel them constructively and clearing space for higher emotions to take root. Freedom lies not in controlling every situation but in mastering our internal settings.

Emotional intelligence encompasses various factors, including individual differences in handling emotions and in particular, the stress that can result from them. People's thresholds for stress vary substantially, and we each employ our own methods for coping. These methods for coping are underpinned by complex physiological and psychological reactions, including hormone releases like cortisol and adrenaline, which prepare the body for a fight or flight response. Stress is not all bad. A certain amount of stress can be beneficial for motivation and performance but when stress exceeds this threshold, it can hinder performance and overwhelm an individual's ability to cope effectively.

In the pursuit of a purposeful life, emotional intelligence serves as a guiding compass, empowering us to navigate the complexities of our inner world and external challenges with clarity and intention. By cultivating self-awareness, we can identify and adjust our emotional bandwidths, amplifying feelings like joy, trust, and compassion while tempering those that hold us back, such as fear or anxiety.

This journey is not about eliminating stress or negative emotions but about harnessing them constructively, using their energy to fuel growth and connection. Through intentional practice and reflection, we can recalibrate our emotional operating systems, creating space for higher emotions to flourish, fostering a life of greater balance, resilience, and meaning.

MOVING FORWARD

The Three Levels of Awareness model offers a roadmap for transforming how we live and connect with others. By recognizing where we stand on this continuum, we gain the power to shift from reactive, fear-driven behaviors to purposeful, love-centered actions.

This journey, inspired by C. Kay Allen and enriched by the teachings of his son, Roger Allen, PhD, on responsibility and cultural change, demands courage and self-awareness but yields a life of deeper meaning and fulfillment. As we commit to aligning our actions with our values, we not only elevate ourselves but also inspire those around us to rise toward Love/Trust, creating a ripple effect of growth and connection.

With this foundation, we are ready to explore the practical tools that bring this awareness to life.

6

Skills for Purposeful Living

LIVING A PURPOSEFUL LIFE MEANS marrying your daily actions with your core values to become the person you desire to be. The journey requires cultivating interpersonal skills that build relationships, resolve conflicts, and orient you toward personal growth. In this chapter, we explore three key skills that elevate you from reactive behaviors rooted in fear or duty to the level of Love/Trust, where compassion and collaboration thrive. These skills are accepting responsibility, active listening, and solution-focused problem solving. Through real-world examples and practical steps, we'll see how they shape your identity and interactions.

MASTERING THREE ESSENTIAL SKILLS

As we've seen, the Three Levels of Awareness model provides a roadmap for understanding how our behaviors impact our relationships and personal growth. At the lowest level, Fear/Anxiety, we react impulsively, maneuvered by mistrust, frustration, or self-preservation. The middle level, Duty/Justice, focuses on obligation and fairness but often lacks empathy or flexibility. The highest level, Love/Trust, is marked by compassion, collaboration, and emotional maturity. Progressing to this level requires mastering three essential skills:

1.   Accepting responsibility for our actions.

2.   Becoming an active, compassionate listener.

3.   Prioritizing solutions over blame.

These skills empower us to pause, reflect, and respond thoughtfully, even under pressure. Fatigue or stress doesn't justify poor behavior. I recall a moment as a young parent when, exhausted after a long day at work, I snapped at my children. "I've had a tough day, so don't push me!" Their quiet stares made me realize I was teaching them that stress excuses harshness. This was a wake-up call. As the adage "Man's extremity is God's opportunity" suggests, challenging moments are opportunities to grow by leaning into our values. By choosing patience over irritation, I began to model the Love/Trust level for my family, reinforcing that our actions determine both our relationships and our character.

Developing these skills is a lifelong practice, so let's delve into each skill and how it contributes to purposeful living.

ACCEPTING RESPONSIBILITY FOR OUR ACTIONS

Accepting responsibility for our actions is crucial, but first responsibility must be properly placed. Assigning responsibility can feel like a game of hot potato, with everyone quick to pass the blame, each one pointing a finger at someone else over mistakes and missteps. Personal integrity means owning your decisions and actions, whether they succeed or fail. Accepting responsibility is how we learn and grow. Properly placing responsibility stimulates healthy, effective relationships while unclaimed personal responsibility causes problems. At work or home, clear agreements about who handles what produce better outcomes. Misunderstandings about responsibilities create confusion and poor results.

Throughout my career, I have found that preempting or resolving issues effectively involves a clear definition and review of responsibilities. Just as in sports, where players who own their responsibilities tend to excel, the same applies in all team settings. And when failure occurs, isolating the issue and evaluating responsibilities appropriately can lead to recovery and improvement.

This principle played out vividly at Key Tronic in the mid-1970s. We were the world's largest keyboard manufacturer, but a new technology, capacitance switches, threatened our market position. Customers kept asking if we had a capacitance switch, and our engineering department kept telling me they couldn't get the proper materials to develop one. Newly developed switches were rumored to cost pennies compared to ours, which cost twenty-five cents, and price was critical to our future.

One of our largest customers, Lear Siegler, had big plans to produce thousands of computer terminals but needed a keyboard priced at twenty-eight dollars, down from our standard thirty-five dollars. I had a good relationship with their chief engineer, Jim Placek, and he wanted to give us the business, an order for ten thousand keyboards. After I muttered, "I'd like to see one of those twenty-eight-dollar keyboards," he handed me one, and I discovered the name of the material supplier.

Seeing an opportunity, I made a bold decision. "Give me the purchase order, and I'll deliver," I promised. Jim trusted me and issued the purchase order. Back at Key Tronic, engineering and purchasing were skeptical. How could we manufacture at that price and stay profitable? Jim Placek had been very clear about his responsibility to purchase keyboards for twenty-eight dollars. And by accepting responsibility for securing the deal, I bridged the gap between the client's needs and our capabilities. I'd researched the material supplier and knew it was feasible. Engineering accepted their share of responsibility and rose to the challenge. Engineering director, Lou Sims, called the vendor and expedited delivery of a sample. Our prototype worked, and after extensive reliability testing, we had a design that assured our ongoing leadership in the keyboard industry.

That order propelled Key Tronic from a $30,000,000 company to a $130,000,000 company. This experience taught me that owning responsibility, even in high-risk situations, can unlock transformative outcomes.

Along with a new technology, the company needed a revised culture. During my absence of eight years, Dad experienced poor health while burning through three CEOs. Without Dad's healthy presence, corporate vision and values became blurred, so people retreated to their individual departments for security. The company fell into a Fear/Anxiety culture, and battles for power erupted.

One of the worst things happened shortly after I returned to the company. Michael Dell came up to me at a trade show. "Are you the new president? I just want to tell you we're dumping you as a supplier for three reasons: quality, quality, and quality!" Things needed to change. I turned to Roger Allen for help, and after he joined us, he did a terrific job teaching skills about communication and taking responsibility. Our quality, communication, and innovation rose.

We developed and even had orders for a new product: a laptop computer. But some old school disgruntled employees convinced the board that laptop computers were a passing phase. So the company and I parted ways, and the new regime intended to clean out everyone loyal to me. Roger was more concerned about me than himself, so eventually, he also got the ax. But we both held to our values, and as it turned out, better opportunities awaited us both.

I love working with troubled youth. Most are honest and willing to take responsibility once they are part of a discussion about actions, consequences, and agreed upon responsibilities based on trust and not accusations. I applied this skill when mentoring a troubled teen named Brad whose mother asked me to talk to him about his declining grades and frequent fights at school.

Our conversation went like this:

"Brad, you're a smart and capable guy. Let's talk about where your life is going," I said when we met.

After a few minutes, I could see he was playing games and not leveling with me, so I got real with him. "Brad, you're not only smart, you also know how to tell the truth. Let's make a deal that you and I will be totally honest with each other."

He agreed, although I had to remind him of his commitment to honesty a few times before he fully accepted it as something he needed to do. I told him I thought he was rebelling and doing some things that weren't in his best interests.

"You're right. I do party," Brad admitted. "And I don't really care about school. I don't like rules. I think my future is football."

I nodded, pleased with his frankness. "I can tell you from personal experience that successful football players abide by rules. So you don't like school and don't think you need an education? Be honest with me here."

"Yeah, I guess I need school, but my teachers aren't any good."

"Okay, let's agree. Your teachers aren't any good. That will be your excuse when you don't graduate?"

"I guess that won't work."

"Okay, Brad, so what do you think you have to do to graduate from school?"

"Well, I can't get into any more fights if I want to stay in school. And I guess I can start studying."

"Paying attention in class and starting to study are going to be tough changes for you. Can you really do it?"

"If I put my mind to it I can."

"Brad, this all sounds good, but what happens when you're tired and the assignment is too hard? Or what happens when someone purposefully tries to start a fight with you? Can you really walk away?"

We continued to talk, and with a little prodding, he finally took responsibility. Then he saw a clear path forward.

Whether in business or personal life, accepting responsibility is the first step toward significant change.

BECOMING AN ACTIVE, COMPASSIONATE LISTENER

Active listening is the foundation of trust and collaboration. It's beyond hearing words. It includes understanding the emotions and intentions behind them. As a parent, for instance, what do you do if your kid comes home and tells you they hate going to school? You may be tempted to be dismissive and authoritarian and say, "You have to go, so deal with it." A better approach is to ask, "Why do you feel that way? What is it about school you don't like?" Open-ended questions invite the child to share and will probably reveal specific issues. But you have to do more than just get them to open up. You have to listen. By listening, you help your child feel *heard*. And that facilitates moving toward solutions.

Active listening follows clear guidelines.

Do:

- Maintain eye contact to show engagement.
- Notice nonverbal cues like body language and facial expressions.
- Put yourself in the speaker's shoes and try to understand their perspective.
- Smile, nod, and allow moments of silence.
- Ask clarifying questions ("Can you tell me more about that?" "What about that is that important to you?")
- Paraphrase to confirm understanding.

Don't:

- Interrupt or finish the speaker's thoughts.
- Use excessive filler words like "uh-huh."
- Hijack the conversation with your own experiences.
- Judge or offer advice prematurely.
- Provide a solution.

Good listeners actively listen to others and pay attention to what is being said. They listen with empathy and without judgment. They ask questions for better understanding and to demonstrate they are engaged in the conversation. This kind of active listening wins over people and creates buy-in before getting into problem-solving.

As a leader, I found that listening actively rather than dictating solutions created trust. When a manager struggled with a project, I'd ask, "What challenges are you facing?" instead of brusquely saying, "Fix it." Or I'd say something like, "What are your key priorities right now and how confident are you of successful outcomes?"

If they were facing challenges or weren't confident about successful outcomes with their key priorities, I would explore options with them. "What do you think you can do to resolve that, and will you need help with it?" If they admitted they needed help, I asked, "What can I do to help?" I often also offered to give them my perceptions on the situation. As we developed a plan, I asked, "What is the best way for you to measure your performance and report to me? And finally, I asked, "Is there anything else you'd like to share with me?" before agreeing on a time frame for talking again.

This approach opened dialogue, uncovered obstacles, and led to collaborative solutions. Helping your associate develop their own solutions provides three valuable benefits: Their problem-solving skills improve, and they're committed. If a solution fails, they own it. It's like teaching someone to fish rather than handing them a fish. And their commitment grows when they discover the answer themselves. Active listening doesn't always solve problems instantly, but it builds trust and lays the groundwork for lasting solutions.

Becoming a *compassionate* active listener doesn't mean letting the other person sidestep responsibility or accepting excuses. Among other things, it means treating them with respect and listening with an ear that acknowledges their humanity. It means seeing employees as more than vehicles to accomplish company goals. It means seeing friends and family members as human beings beyond the roles they play in your life.

It also means listening for what others do right and acknowledging it. I'm always looking for ways to compliment others, and it's remarkable how much it impacts both them and me. Complimenting someone means truly seeing them and making an effort to connect. When we focus solely on ourselves, we spiral into worry, hurt, and self-absorption. But when we shift our attention outward, the world feels brighter. Stay alert for chances to offer a kind word or a small favor. We all crave recognition, and a sincere compliment can instantly create a bond.

If you want to be surrounded by people who value you, start by valuing them through simple acts of kindness, compassion, and encouragement—whether it's your kids, spouse, colleagues, or a stranger. Great leaders, coaches, and parents don't dwell on mistakes. They celebrate what you do right.

I volunteered with Big Brothers Big Sisters of America, mentoring a boy who faced bullying at school and neglect at home. When I picked him up, his sadness and low confidence were clear. We'd spend time together, and I made a point of listening to him, interacting with him, and complimenting him. After a few hours, I'd see him walk taller, his spirit lifted. But the moment we returned to his house, his mother's criticism would erase that confidence, and his posture returned to a slump. It was a stark reminder of the power of words.

One day, I decided to do something lasting. I picked him up from school and we confronted his bullies together. We talked it out, and that included active listening to what the bullies had to say. It worked, and they left him alone after that.

Want to spread some cheer? Ask yourself how many compliments you've given today. I've been having fun telling waiters, "You have such a great way with people," or cashiers, "You're so quick. Your boss must love you." These small gestures make them smile, but they make me feel even better. Try setting a daily goal: Compliment ten people. With kids, a spouse, coworkers, and strangers, you'll easily encounter dozens of opportunities. It might take three minutes total, but it'll leave them—and you—happier. Compliments are free, limitless, and contagious.

Maya Angelou is often credited with saying, "People will forget what you said, people will forget what you did, but they will never forget how you made them feel" although evidence suggests a version of this quote was first attributed to Carl W. Buehner, a leader in the Church of Jesus Christ of Latter-day Saints. Regardless of the original source, a compliment about someone's sweater might fade from memory, but the warmth you create endures.

Insecure leaders, especially younger ones, often withhold praise. Most haven't learned how to listen actively and compassionately. And they're too caught up in self-doubt. But secure, confident leaders listen actively and freely give compliments, wielding a powerful, free tool. Companies obsess over profits, yet this simple act of recognition—a currency that costs nothing—can transform relationships and build lasting value.

Prioritizing Solutions Over Blame

Blaming others escalates conflicts; focusing on solutions builds bridges. When addressing an issue, share your perspective objectively ("I've noticed . . .") and invite collaboration ("Can we find a solution?"). This approach develops teamwork without undermining the other person's confidence.

Constructive problem solving follows seven steps:

1. **Choose the right time to talk.** You don't want to engage in a serious conversation when the other person is distracted or rushed.

2. **Build trust.** Affirm the relationship's value. ("You and I have known each other for a long time, and we share the same goals.") Confirm that you are not in opposition even if you have different perceptions.

3. **State the issue.** Express your feelings without blame. ("I'm feeling concerned about . . .") Objectively share how you feel without suggesting the other person *makes* you feel that way.

4. **Acknowledge differing views.** Ask, "How do you see this?" Be open to other perspectives without becoming offended, defensive, or lapsing into blame.

5. **Invite solutions.** Invite the other person to brainstorm with you. ("What can we do to address this? How can we find an answer that works for both of us?") The solution has to come from them. If you provide the solution, there's no ownership commitment to make it happen.

6. **Confirm agreement.** Summarize to ensure mutual understanding.

7. **Build resolve.** Once we have commitment, we need to talk about the potential roadblocks they might have to overcome and how to anticipate challenges. We also need to develop appropriate responses to roadblocks and challenges.

By focusing on constructive problem solving and taking responsibility, we cultivate a mindset that not only resolves challenges but also clarifies our purpose. This shift from blame to ownership prompts reflection on our broader aspirations, guiding us to consider not just what we want to achieve, but who we want to become.

SHOW VULNERABILITY

Leaders often cling to the myth of unwavering strength, believing they must always appear confident and infallible. True leadership lies in embracing vulnerability, fallibility, and humility. Those trapped in the myth of strength often become hardened, arrogant, or paranoid, making poor decisions driven by insecurity and a need to prove themselves. I once received a powerful compliment: "Fred doesn't have to prove anything." It reminded me that authentic leadership isn't about projecting invincibility but about focusing on others, whether those others are employees, clients, friends, or family members.

Admitting vulnerability can feel counterintuitive (particularly for men), but it builds trust and respect. By acknowledging our stumbles, we shift the focus from self to others, which is the heart of leadership. And by acknowledging that we are fully human and therefore capable of being wounded, we avoid the fallacy of invincibility and become infinitely more relatable. (Even superheroes have vulnerabilities, their personal kryptonite.) My father modeled this beautifully at Key Tronic, where he ran the company on a "grapevine" model. He listened to everyone, from janitors to directors, openly admitting when he didn't have all the answers. For instance, he told investment bankers, "You understand our finances better than we do. That's why we need your advice." His willingness to be vulnerable fostered openness, earning him trust and invaluable insights.

I learned this lesson myself at Key Tronic after I placed a large order for keyboards and there was a special connector we needed to get. Trying to cut costs, I ordered the same amount as the customer's initial blanket order. But they changed the connector they used, leaving us with useless and expensive inventory. Our director of mechanical engineering confronted me. "We're tight on money, and we have all this inventory we don't need. Everything you touch turns to shit."

Instead of reacting defensively, I tried something new and chose vulnerability. "Larry, I have great respect for you, and I'm doing my best. I don't know what to say, because I want to perform in a way *you* will respect."

To my surprise, Larry broke down, apologized, and shared that he was in a bad mood, struggling through a divorce. That moment taught me the power of vulnerability—not just in admitting my mistake but in creating space for others to open up. Larry and I both shared our vulnerability.

When leaders show vulnerability, they lead by example, encouraging others to do the same. It develops connection, trust, and collaboration. My challenge to leaders is simple: Let go of the need to appear unbreakable. Embrace vulnerability.

Overwhelmed with two financial responsibilities, I once sat with my staff, bemoaning my situation and workload. I decided to list my responsibilities and ask if anyone wanted to take some of them. A new energy entered the conference room as associates picked up some of my load. We all left the room excited about the new division of responsibilities. By allowing others to see my vulnerability, we all benefited.

VISUALIZING OUR DESTINATION

Many of us meticulously plan our finances, fitness, and careers but overlook defining the person we want to become. Without this vision, we risk reacting to life's challenges rather than shaping our destiny. We focus on short-term demands rather than long-term goals. As I've mentioned, my father, a driven leader at Key Tronic, embodied honesty and productivity but tied his identity to work. When he retired, he felt displaced and depressed, struggling to find purpose. Only later did he discover joy in *being*—connecting with family and reflecting on his legacy—rather than *doing*. This shift underlines a truth: Purpose lies in becoming, not achieving. Dad lived out his final years appreciating who he *was* and who he was becoming.

Think of your vision as a fly-by-wire system in aviation, where pilots set their destination before takeoff and trust the system to automatically adapt to changing conditions to keep them on course. Similarly, defining who you want to be (for instance, compassionate, trustworthy, resilient) keeps you on course.

Visualizing your destination requires introspection. Ask some questions: What values define me? Who do I admire, and why? How do I want to be remembered? These questions anchor your purpose, guiding you through stress or setbacks. In my faith community, members often look to revered figures for inspiration, striving to embody their qualities. Whatever your beliefs, a clear vision of your "enlightened" self—the part of you that receives and embraces the "light" this kind of inspiration provides—ensures your actions reflect your highest aspirations. Eating, playing, working, and all the other "ings" are temporary gratifications, but our purpose is to arrive at *being*.

LIVING VALUES IN ACTION

At Key Tronic, my father's passion for handheld optical character readers (OCRs), magic wands that read numbers, tested my ability to live my values. It happened not long after Lew Jr. saved the company and we'd built up a cash surplus. Dad saw OCRs as an excellent investment, a revolutionary input method alongside our keyboards. None of us had seen anything like it before, and Dad enthusiastically presented the technology to our managers, telling them we were going to buy it. The managers nodded in agreement, but I recognized their reluctance to challenge him. Most of them had learned to nod and stay out of his way when he was excitedly heading down a certain path. It was clear to me he was investing in a technology without knowing exactly what we were going to do with it.

When nobody asked probing questions (like "What's the market?" or "What's the application?"), my value of honesty said it was up to me to be candid with him. I took him to one side and said, "Dad, if this fails, no one will admit they supported it."

He studied me for a moment, and instead of commenting on the lemming mentality of his employees asked, "Are you getting cold feet?"

"I don't know about that," I replied, "but I'd like them to be a bit warmer."

The next day, Dad walked into my office and said, "I want you to set up and run our OCR division."

Whether he was testing my commitment to the company, giving me the incentive I needed, or both, I didn't know, but I didn't have to think about my answer. It was an opportunity to run a division on my own and establish a professional identity separate from his. I grabbed it with both hands.

Finding an application for the OCR wasn't easy. After months of research, we found a problem to solve. Banks needed a faster way to process credit card receipts, so pairing the OCR with a document transport vastly outpaced their long, laborious process of manually shuffling receipts and keying in numbers. Banks placed sizeable orders, and the division became extremely profitable. Years later, during a slump in keyboard demand, the OCR division carried the company. Living my values of candor and responsibility turned a risky venture into a triumph.

Buoyed by my success, I suggested Dad promote me to executive VP of the entire company, and he agreed. But at the start of the next weekly meeting, I saw the managers look around, waiting for him to appear. They hadn't been informed of my new position! Without Dad's dynamic presence, they were uneasy, and the meeting sputtered along as they participated in a desultory, half-hearted manner.

The managers were hesitant to accept me as their leader. But one little book changed the dynamics of our meetings and increased their accountability. In the past, we'd never taken meeting minutes and hadn't followed up on prior commitments, so I began to log commitments in an imposing, leather-bound book.

Out of habit, a manager would commit, but then, as I wrote it down, he'd say, "Wait. Are you putting that in your book?"

"Yes, so that's your commitment, right?" I'd reply.

Formalizing their assurance by writing it down in the book made them seriously consider what they were doing. "Well, if it's going in the book, let me think about it for a minute," they would frequently say next.

I was executing my value of placing responsibility properly. And the manager knew he would have to honor his obligation.

Dad tried to be supportive but couldn't let go. By stepping aside, he felt at a loss. What else could he do with his life? Everything revolved around work. I sold him part of my ranch, thinking he'd find fulfillment there, but that didn't work. So he sometimes walked into the office and made casual suggestions. But a casual suggestion from the founder meant "Do it." He'd spent years as a wise, powerful leader many admired and some feared. Every time he walked into a room, it was immediately obvious who the real boss was.

While I was working on becoming a better manager, my skills were not sufficient to handle the tricky issue of apportioning responsibility for running the company between myself and my father. I had not reached the Love/Trust level. The conflict between Dad and I over who should run the company was building to a climax that would ultimately leave just one of us in charge.

He fired me! This underscored the critical need to develop stronger interpersonal skills, not only to manage my relationship with him but also to boost trust and collaboration with our workforce. These skills became the foundation for developing more effective and rewarding connections, both personally and professionally.

INTERPERSONAL SKILLS FOR CONNECTION

The key interpersonal skills that can help form and nurture rewarding relationships are openness, empathy, avoiding issuing blame, and candor. Here's how:

- **Openness.** Admit mistakes and welcome feedback to engender trust. Openness invites transparency and stirs a meaningful connection between individuals.
- **Empathy.** Understand the perspectives of others to bridge divides. Empathetic communication is a central part of conflict resolution.
- **Avoid blame.** Let others express concerns without judgment. Finger-pointing is a guaranteed way to create and prolong friction.
- **Candor.** Speak honestly with humility and compassion. People respect those willing to speak the truth, but it's vital to do so tactfully.

TOOLS FOR LIFE

The skills of responsibility, active and compassionate listening, and solution-focused problem solving, equip you to handle life's complexities with grace when you combine them with living your values. They channel you from Fear/Anxiety to Love/Trust, enhancing relationships and personal growth. Visualizing who you want to become links your actions with your aspirations, ensuring a life of purpose, not just achievement.

At breakfast one day, my son Isaiah, seven years old at the time, remarked that I was more fun after leaving Key Tronic, revealing how my workaholic focus had negatively impacted the family. I sought to justify the hours. "Well, Isaiah, my work was very demanding, but I was doing it for our family."

His mother was not going to let me get away with that and gently disagreed, noting that my primary motivation was the drive to turn around the company and become a force in the industry. She was right. Rather than the money I was bringing in, my family needed my time. I could have balanced both, but like my father before me, I prioritized work. This lesson reinforced that purpose transcends tasks. It's about embodying love, trust, and integrity.

I learned the hard way, but you can make it easy on yourself by employing the skills I've discussed. They serve as pivotal instruments for crafting a purposeful existence, guiding us from merely reacting to life's challenges to actively shaping our destinies. They elevate our interactions and personal growth.

To live purposefully, reflect on your values daily. Listen to your inner voice. Ask some questions: Am I acting with compassion? Am I listening to understand? Am I solving problems collaboratively? These questions lock you to your vision, even in turbulent times. Whether mentoring youth, leading a team, or nurturing family, these skills build a fulfilling life. By applying them consistently, you become the person you want to be, equipped to face the future with clarity, confidence, and purpose. I've learned that in quiet moments on my knees, I can effectively pause, reflect, and open my mind to inspiration and guidance.

This daily commitment to values not only influences one's actions but also forges a deeper sense of self, defined by integrity and connection. The practice of compassion, understanding, and collaboration lays the groundwork for a life of meaning, but it is their transformation into enduring virtues that truly anchors your purpose. As these qualities become second nature, they guide us toward a legacy beyond just achievements, one of character and relationships that stand the test of time.

7

Embracing Key Moments for Personal Growth

THE PURSUIT OF VIRTUES IS a lifelong journey, one that turns us into better versions of ourselves. In the process, we become more compassionate family members, reliable friends, inspiring leaders, and considerate colleagues. This journey is not a sprint but a marathon requiring consistent effort and unwavering commitment to our values. Growth is not a one-time achievement. It demands vigilance, because complacency can erode even the strongest principles.

Key moments, those critical junctures when our decisions carry lasting consequences, test our ability to uphold and refine our virtues. Righteous virtues emerge when we resist temptations, overcome distractions, and choose the path of integrity over convenience. When we internalize our values as virtues and both recognize and navigate key moments with mindfulness and purpose, we not only substantially improve ourselves but also inspire those around us to strive for their best selves.

THE NATURE OF KEY MOMENTS

While major life decisions like choosing a career, selecting a life partner, or making a sizeable financial investment can be key moments, more often than not, key moments can be seemingly minor choices, like addressing a workplace conflict or resisting an unhealthy indulgence. Regardless of their scale, these moments share a common trait: They are impactful events during which we can either let our emotions rule the roost or choose to let our values drive our behavior. Often, they arrive unexpectedly, igniting emotions such as anger, fear, frustration, or jealousy that threaten to cloud our judgment and derail our principles.

Uncontrolled emotions can shut down rational thinking, distance us from solutions, and damage relationships. For example, a heated argument with a colleague might tempt us to lash out, prioritizing short-term satisfaction over long-term trust. Similarly, yielding to a moment of weakness, such as indulging in a detrimental habit like overeating junk food, may seem inconsequential, but repeated lapses can undermine our goals. Recognizing key moments is essential because it allows us to pause, reflect, and choose responses that reflect our aspirations rather than our impulses.

The old saying "Don't let the emotion make the decision" captures a timeless piece of wisdom: the importance of thoughtful deliberation over impulsive action. While emotions are integral to our experiences, mastering them is crucial to ensuring they aid rather than obstruct our decision-making processes. By managing our emotions and connecting them with our values, we minimize errors resulting from actions based on raw feelings and maximize actions that reflect our true intentions.

The stakes in key moments are high. Our choices influence our habits, relationships, and sense of self. A single decision to act with integrity can reinforce our moral foundation, while a lapse can erode trust and self-respect and even ruin relationships. By cultivating self-awareness and emotional intelligence, we equip ourselves to convert challenges into opportunities for growth.

THE POWER OF LIVED VALUES

Values alone are not enough. They must be practiced and tested in real-life situations to become internalized virtues. Like muscles, virtues grow stronger when exercised against resistance. When we exercise our virtue muscles, we consciously choose the *harder right* over the *easier wrong*. Key moments provide the opportunity to practice virtue resistance training, thereby solidifying our principles. When self-interest, fear, or external pressures push us toward compromise or in other difficult moments, we have a chance to prove our commitment to integrity.

Our actions also serve as a model for others, subtly affecting their behavior and fostering a culture of mutual respect and trust. For instance, a leader who consistently demonstrates fairness and empathy in high-pressure situations inspires their team to do the same. Similarly, a parent who models patience and honesty in everyday interactions instills those qualities in their children and subsequent generations. By living our values, we create genuine relationships that reinforce the bonds that matter most.

This ripple effect underscores the importance of consistency. Virtues are not defined by isolated acts of heroism but by the steady accumulation of principled choices. Each key moment we handle with integrity strengthens our character and amplifies our influence, contributing to a more ethical and compassionate world.

LESSONS FROM PERSONAL EXPERIENCE

Early in my career, I struggled to embody the virtues I now cherish. I was sometimes an oppressive boss and didn't consistently base my behavior on my moral compass. I can now see why I had those struggles. As a young manager, I faced relentless pressure to save and then grow the business. In the chaos of deadlines and challenges, I sometimes lost sight of my basic values of fairness, humility, and compassion. I was reactive rather than intentional, occasionally intimidating colleagues instead of inspiring them. These shortcomings were most evident in key moments when stress blurred my judgment, causing me to prioritize results over relationships.

Over time, I learned that managing with empathy, humility, and compassion for others yielded far better outcomes for all parties. By prioritizing the well-being of others and listening to their perspectives, I reduced my own stress and cultivated a more positive workplace culture. Decision-making became clearer, relationships deepened, and productivity soared. This transformation reinforced a critical lesson: Words alone do not create culture. Right action must accompany the words.

True leadership, whether in business or personal life, is built on a foundation of lived values, not just spoken ideals. This focus on lived values carries over to how we face challenges. By approaching trials with the same empathy and integrity that define effective leadership, we turn obstacles into opportunities for personal growth.

TRIALS AS CATALYSTS FOR GROWTH

Trials and temptations are not obstacles to be avoided but opportunities to be embraced. They test our moral agency, our ability and freedom to choose between what we consider to be right and wrong. That may come in the form of choosing either self-interest or a greater good. It may be an occasion where we must choose between long-term integrity and temporary satisfaction. Each key moment presents a battle between the forces of good and evil. One path leads to growth, wisdom, and ethical behavior. The other leads to short-lived pleasure, complacency, selfishness, and short-term gain. Our responses in these moments shape our personal development and define the person we are becoming.

Rather than viewing trials as burdens, we should see them as catalysts for refining our virtues. Every challenge—whether a professional setback, a personal conflict, or an ethical dilemma—offers a chance to strengthen our moral foundation. For example, choosing to address a workplace issue head-on, despite the discomfort, builds courage and fosters trust. Resisting the urge to cut corners on a project reinforces integrity and self-discipline.

Mindfulness plays a central role in this process. By observing our emotions and reflecting on our values, we gain the wisdom needed to *act* thoughtfully rather than *react* impulsively. As Roger Allen, wisely noted, "A soft answer means you respond to what is happening from a deeper, quieter, more grounded place. You don't need to react—you can choose."

This approach allows us to take control of our decisions, ensuring they live up to our highest aspirations. Socrates' phrase "know thyself" holds profound value, encouraging us to step outside ourselves, observe our actions, and gain real insight into our own nature and the people around us.

A DEFINING MOMENT

One of the most consequential key moments in my life occurred in the 1970s. I spoke of this event earlier, but I'm expanding on it here because it truly was a defining moment.

While I'd contributed significantly to our company's growth, enhanced operations, and drove innovation, working under my father's imposing presence created ongoing tensions because our roles often overlapped. Frustrated, I confronted him one day, keeping my voice steady despite my internal turmoil. "Dad, we're stepping on each other's toes. It might be best for one of us to step back."

He listened quietly and suggested I take a week off while he considered a solution.

In my mind, the resolution was clear: At sixty-eight, my father was near retirement age, and I was ready to take over. I retreated to my ranch to formulate my leadership priorities, confident I would soon assume control of the company. At the end of the week, Dad drove out to meet me. We settled on the lawn, the sprawling landscape offering a deceptive calm that belied the impending storm.

His words blindsided me. "I've decided to fire you." His tone was both regretful and firm. "I'm not sure what you should do. Maybe sell cars."

The news hit like a thunderbolt, even though the feeling behind the words was *I hate to do this to you, kid*. I wondered if he'd even considered retiring. Not only was he not retiring, but I was out of a job. I assumed he'd conducted an informal survey among the managers, asking who should run the company, and the majority had expressed greater confidence in his continued leadership. Unlike me, they must also have realized Dad was simply not ready to retire.

Financial security became an immediate concern, and I suggested selling my shares only to have Dad dismiss their value. Reeling from the shock, I resolved to find another buyer. An investment banking firm valued my stock at two million dollars, an offer Key Tronic matched. Though the financial resolution provided relief, the emotional and professional toll was immense. I questioned my worth and wrestled with uncertainty. I had no idea what I was going to do now that I been fired from Key Tronic.

Reflecting on those conversations, I recognized that my shortfall in interpersonal skills and strategic communication, especially in key moments, contributed to the outcome. Had I been equipped with the emotional intelligence and leadership skills I now teach, perhaps we could have navigated the situation collaboratively, guiding Key Tronic to greater heights. Instead, my father's decision led to a decade of instability for the company, marked by senior management changes (running through three presidents), personal health struggles for my dad, and declining profits.

This adversity became a crossroads. Rather than succumbing to self-pity, after a reflective hiatus at my ranch, I channeled my energy into new business ventures, immersing myself in years of relentless activity. (Idleness has never suited me.) While not all my endeavors succeeded, they enriched my professional experience and taught me resilience. In retrospect, Dad may have thought firing me was the best thing for me. And in some ways, it was.

Most importantly, I dedicated myself to mastering the people management skills I had lacked. When I rejoined Key Tronic a decade later, I was a transformed leader, adept at navigating complex interpersonal dynamics and fostering collaboration. This challenging period reinforced a powerful truth: Adversity, when faced head-on, can be a catalyst for personal and professional growth.

STRATEGIES FOR NAVIGATING KEY MOMENTS

To seize key moments as opportunities for growth, we must approach them with intention and discipline. The following strategies should be pursued:

1. **Clarify Your Values.** A well-defined understanding of your core beliefs provides a compass for decision-making. Take time to

articulate what matters most to you—whether it's honesty, compassion, service, or other values—and let these principles guide your responses in critical situations.

2. **Identify Emotional Triggers.** Develop self-awareness by recognizing when emotions like anger, insecurity, jealousy, or fear surface. These feelings often signal a key moment, alerting you to pause and respond thoughtfully rather than react impulsively.

3. **Acknowledge Multiple Key Moments.** Complex situations may present several pivotal moments. For example, a workplace conflict might involve an initial disagreement, a follow-up discussion, and a resolution process. Stay patient and compassionate, holding fast to your values throughout.

4. **Refine Interpersonal Skills.** Enhance your ability to listen actively, withhold judgment, and express genuine care. Seek resolutions that prioritize the well-being of all parties, fomenting trust, and collaboration.

THE ROLE OF MINDFULNESS, CONSCIENCE, AND CHOOSING THE HIGHER PATH

Mindfulness is a cornerstone of mastering key moments. By stepping back from the chaos of intense emotions, we create space to evaluate our options and harmonize our actions with our principles. A simple technique, slowing your breathing for ninety seconds, can shift you from a reactive state to a responsive one. That promotes lucidity and emotional intelligence, ensuring your decisions reflect your values.

Equally important is tuning in to our conscience, that inner voice that channels us toward goodness. Often experienced as internal promptings or subtle nudges, I perceive it as spiritual guidance, recognized in religions and wisdom traditions as the Holy Spirit, Ilham, or Higher Self. These quiet yet powerful promptings often manifest as gentle whispers urging us toward goodness: "Help her with the groceries," "Hold your temper," or "Resist the allure of temptation." Conversely, there are destructive forces that seek to derail our virtuous endeavors, sometimes named as Satan, Shytan, or Mara.

Life is a constant tug-of-war between these positive promptings and destructive forces—whether labeled as temptation, ego, or self-gratification. For me, The Three Levels of Awareness model has been a revelation, a framework for traversing this inner battlefield.

- **Level 1: Selfish Impulses.** Overwhelmed by raw emotions, we react impulsively, prioritizing personal gain over principles.
- **Level 2: Tempered Awareness.** With restraint, we respond with greater awareness, balancing emotions and values.
- **Level 3: Higher Perspective.** Rising above fleeting feelings, we act with wisdom, compassion, and purpose.

In key moments, this model serves as a mirror, reflecting our current state and guiding us toward Level 3. By consistently aligning our actions with this highest level, we transcend emotional whims, using our feelings as catalysts for growth and fulfillment.

Key moments are like forks in the road, offering a choice between two distinct paths. One path, fueled by impulsive reactions, leads to contention, fractured relationships, and short-term victories won at the expense of peace. The other, higher path ascends to wisdom, thoughtful problem-solving, and genuine connections with others. Choosing the latter requires discipline, patience, and an unwavering commitment to personal growth. Yet it is a choice that radically changes not only us but the world around us.

Each thoughtful response in a key moment is a step toward our ideal self. These victories—however small—build resilience, bolster trust, and contribute to a life of purpose. The question is not whether key moments will arise. They are inevitable waypoints in life's journey. The real question is how we will respond when they do.

As discussed earlier, too often, we drift through life, reacting to events rather than intentionally shaping our path. We let outside circumstances, such as a rude comment or a professional disappointment, control our emotions. But why should someone else's behavior dictate our inner state? Why give that power away? We're not helpless. When we become aware of the opposing forces within us—our higher conscience and our emotional impulses—we realize we can choose. We can respond with intention rather than react by default.

Every decision we make plays a part in who we are becoming. While we have the freedom to respond however we wish, we are never free from the consequences of those responses. Living with purpose means owning our choices (our thoughts, emotions, and behaviors) and ensuring they reflect the person we aspire to be. Life's challenges will come, but we can use them to grow stronger. Rather than letting adversity steer us off course, we can harness it, letting it push us forward, toward greater character, purpose, and meaning.

A CALL TO ACTION

Life is defined by key moments, and those pivotal junctures test our values and offer us the chance to grow. When asked what values we should seek to develop as virtues, I reply, "First, ask how you can best serve someone else." Growth begins with service, not self-interest. Virtues often take root in our interactions with others, especially during moments of challenge. Observing someone act with integrity, humility, or compassion can inspire us to rise to that same standard.

Ultimately, a purposeful life isn't defined by the absence of hardship but by the wisdom and courage with which we respond to it. We have the opportunity to be the architects of our own fortune—one decision, one moment at a time. We're not judged solely by past actions. We're also judged by the people we are today. For people of faith, that final judgment lies with the Creator. But regardless of belief, the message is the same: Reflect, act with purpose, and know that becoming better is always within reach.

8

Reviewing Your Values and Behavior

SELF-REFLECTION IS A CORNERSTONE OF a meaningful life. It constitutes a deliberate act of stepping back from the whirlwind of daily demands to examine who we are, what we stand for, and whether our actions conform to our aspirations. It's not a one-time event but a habit, a rhythm that keeps us tethered to our purpose. Let's explore how to review our values, refine our behavior, and pursue a life of authenticity. This will include how to weave together practical tools like self-reflection, mindfulness, the power of external perspectives, becoming a detective when you feel discomfort, and hard-earned lessons from personal victories and missteps.

From a young age, I wanted to live a life I could look back on with pride, filled with meaningful and productive achievements. But somewhere along the way, I lost my path. College was tough, a harsh environment where I learned that sharp wit and sarcasm could shield me from cruelty. My athletic background taught me to push through opposition with force, and I carried that mindset into my post-college life. In business, I approached challenges like a sports match, throwing all my energy into defeating the "opponent." Negotiations became a win-lose battle, not a collaborative win-win effort.

My combative, aggressive behavior stemmed from a defense mechanism rooted in survival mode. When I felt threatened, I lashed out, much like a cornered animal. I've since realized that true confidence comes from higher-level behavior, not fear-driven, self-focused thinking. When you're secure in yourself, you don't feel threatened. You can offer boundless kindness without losing strength. This applies to all relationships, including those with family. Instead of reacting defensively to an offense, you can approach it with understanding and help others navigate their struggles.

Over time, I saw how much my emotions and competitive nature controlled my interactions. I learned life doesn't have to be a constant contest. This realization led me to embrace self-reflection, a practice that helped me chart a better course.

Self-reflection is a rare skill in today's world. We're often so focused on gaining recognition that we overlook our flaws. But a wise person stays mindful of their weaknesses, not to dwell on them but to consciously improve. Like any worthwhile pursuit, it demands discipline and commitment.

One effective way to practice self-reflection is to have a conversation with an imaginary life coach who fosters self-awareness by asking targeted questions. These are the kinds of questions we should ask ourselves to grow:

- Review your purpose. How are you making this world a better place?
- What relationships can you improve? How?
- How have your time and talents helped those around you?
- What virtues make up your purpose?
- Do your actions confirm your intentions?
- How do your daily priorities, activities, and interactions project your purpose?
- Looking back at this week's interactions with individuals, were you aware of their feelings? Did you lighten their load (concerns) in any way?
- What thoughts or actions were out of character? Have you repented (turned away)? If not, how can you improve?

- What virtues and what weaknesses are you focusing on this week?
- List three people you want to lift up this week through deed or voice.
- List three things that must be part of your ideal role or job and three things that must not be a part of it.
- What has your life experience taught you about your destiny?
- Which relationships or individuals have shaped your sense of purpose, and how?
- How has your culture or community influenced your sense of purpose?

THE ART AND DISCIPLINE OF REVIEWING VALUES

To live according to our values requires more than vague intentions. It calls for clarity and consistency. One of the most actionable ways to cultivate this is through a structured review, a practice that has roots in history. Picture Benjamin Franklin, stuck on a creaking ship crossing the Atlantic for thirteen weeks in 1726. Boredom could have dulled his mind. It didn't. He turned the voyage into a laboratory for self-improvement. Franklin penned a personal list of thirteen virtues: temperance, silence, order, resolution, frugality, industry, sincerity, justice, moderation, cleanliness, tranquility, chastity, and humility. He devoted a week to mastering each, meticulously noting his progress in a pocket journal.

We can borrow from Franklin's playbook. Imagine setting aside an hour each week, perhaps a quiet Sunday evening, in your favorite "quiet place." You may have a notebook with you or you may choose to just sit with your thoughts. During this reflective time, ask yourself some questions: Did I live with integrity this week? Did I honor my priorities? Where am I strong? Where do I need to stretch?

This isn't flogging yourself for your shortcomings but taking stock. It's a way to ensure you're heading toward the person you envision for yourself.

Values don't morph into virtues by accident. They're fashioned through repetition and reflection, often over decades. Think of it like learning a craft—woodworking, playing the piano, or anything else—where mastery derives from years of practice. Regularly revisiting your values, whether through a formal ritual like Franklin's or a quick mental pause before a momentous choice, builds those skills.

My father-in-law, Mark Willis, embodies this beautifully. A titan in business—president of the Federal Reserve Bank of Minneapolis, president of General Mills, chairman and CEO of *Times Mirror* in Los Angeles—he never let ambition eclipse what mattered most to him: faith, family, and service. Curious, I once asked him the secret behind his work-life balance. "You may not have a balanced day or even a balanced week," he replied, "but you can have a balanced life." When business trips or boardroom crises pulled him away, he doubled down later, carving out extra hours for his wife, his kids, and the church. His approach was simple yet profound: Keep your values in sight and let them dictate how you spend your time, even when the world pulls you in a dozen directions.

I've tripped where he strode. Early in my own life, I didn't guard my values fiercely enough. Emotions blurred them. I'd make snap decisions that felt right in the heat of the moment only to realize later that they clashed with what I claimed to hold dear. If I'd paused to review those values, holding them up like a lantern, and regularly reviewed them, I might have sidestepped those detours. The lesson seared into me. Again and again, we must ask ourselves these two questions: What do I stand for? Is it shaping my choices?

For some, values spring from conscience, that quiet voice nudging us toward rightness. For others, they're a divine gift of the spirit, bestowed through faith or revelation. For many, it's both. Whatever their source, they require our attention. We need to work on harmonizing our actions with our beliefs. We must cultivate awareness, crafting a vivid vision of who we want to be, not a vague silhouette but a detailed portrait. That vision becomes our North Star, especially in moments of crisis or temptation, guiding us when instinct alone might lead us astray.

EXTERNAL PERSPECTIVES

We're unreliable narrators of our own stories. I see myself through the rosy filter of my intentions: I know I mean well. Others see the raw footage of my actions, unedited and sometimes unflattering. Bridging this gap takes guts. It means inviting feedback from those who know us best. Imagine sitting across from your spouse over lunch or calling a close friend and asking some tough questions, which may include one or more of the following: How do you see me? What do I put out into the world? What do people think of me?

Once you've asked, brace yourself. Don't argue or deflect. Practice active listening and absorb what they have to say. You're not handing them the gavel to judge you, but you *are* borrowing their lens to spot what you might miss. Don't defend yourself. If you do, the discussion will likely end.

Take a workplace example. A manager gathers her team and asks, "How can I lead you better?"

She might do this expecting a pat on the back only to have a junior colleague speak candidly. "You're great at strategy, but you cut people off when they're pitching ideas."

The manager's intent during meetings where team members feel cut off might be efficiency. She just wants to keep the meeting on track. But the impact is exclusion, at least from the eyes of the colleague who gave her that frank feedback. It would not be fun to hear, but it would be a gift. Feedback isn't a binding contract. Some of it misses the mark, colored by the biases of those giving it. A friend might call you aloof when you're just introspective. Sift it carefully. You decide what is in keeping with your values, but even the off-target stuff can spur a useful question: Is there a kernel of truth here?

At the end of the day, you're the arbiter. No one else can climb inside your soul and weigh your fidelity to your principles. But the perspectives of others help us see the gap between the "me" we intend and the "me" we project—a gap we can close with intention and effort. If you are sincere enough to ask others to evaluate whether you are truly living your values, my guess is you already know what you need to work on.

SELF-REFLECTION: THE ART OF GAINING PERSPECTIVE

Self-reflection, a timeless practice embraced across cultures, offers a powerful way to step back and observe our thoughts, emotions, and actions with clarity and detachment. At its core, it is about pausing, creating a gap between what happens to us and how we choose to respond. It's like watching yourself from a distance, free from the pull of immediate reactions.

This practice takes many forms. Sometimes it is as simple as slowing your breath, releasing tension, or picturing a calm scene, such as a quiet stream winding through a forest. Other times it is more analytical: taking a fifty-thousand-foot view of your life and choices or zooming in with a microscopic lens on a single decision, behavior, or value. It may be asking yourself questions such as:

- Does my behavior align with my values?
- How will I handle this challenge?
- Why did I react that way?
- What am I really trying to accomplish?
- How might others—my colleagues, family, and community—see this situation?

I discovered self-reflection long before I knew its name. In moments of doubt, I'd find a quiet space and imagine a conversation with a trusted mentor or a higher power.

"How are you doing?" the voice would ask.

"Fine," I'd say, casual as ever.

"How are you *really* doing?" the voice would counter.

That's when the walls would come down. I'd pour out my fears, frustrations, and flickering hopes, sifting through them with a clearer mind. Insights would surface. Maybe a grudge to let go, a choice to reconsider, a gratitude to embrace. I'd emerge lighter, as if I'd shed a burden.

But reflection doesn't always need a mentor, imagined or real. Sometimes it's simply about thinking deeply. It might be reviewing the day's conversations, replaying moments of tension to see where you could have listened better or spoken with more empathy. It might be analyzing whether your current path aligns with your core values or whether the goals you're pursuing are truly your own. This reflective analysis sharpens self-awareness and makes your actions more deliberate.

Self-reflection is also relational. It means holding up a mirror not only to your inner world but also to the way your choices ripple outward. How might a decision affect my team? How might my behavior look from my spouse's perspective? How might my assumptions fit—or clash—with the broader culture I live in? This shift in vantage point widens one's perspective and reduces blind spots.

For those rooted in a spiritual tradition, self-reflection can take on another dimension: examining how one's actions and intentions align with sacred teachings. A Christian might ask themselves if they're living out the commandment to love their neighbor. A Muslim might reflect on whether daily actions embody the mercy of Allah. A Buddhist may ask whether a response comes from compassion or attachment. This spiritual reflection adds a transcendent anchor, reminding us that our choices are not just personal but part of a larger moral and spiritual fabric. Moments of quiet reflection allow the inner voice to be heard.

Reflection is not confined to quiet moments of solitude. It's a practical tool for navigating life's pressures. Imagine a heated exchange with a colleague. What if you paused, even for a heartbeat, to ask yourself if you would choose different words if you knew someone you deeply respect were watching. That pause can change the course of a conversation, transforming conflict into collaboration.

Over time, self-reflection becomes less a practice and more a way of being. It loosens the ego's grip and trains us to see ourselves honestly—our strengths and shortcomings, our progress and patterns. It cultivates humility, empathy, and resilience. In short, self-reflection is not just about looking inward, it is also about gaining perspective from within, from without, and from above. It is a lifelong art that shapes the way we live, love, and lead.

TRIALS AS TEACHERS

We're born with a raw, untamed side with emotions like anger and envy and appetites for comfort and acclaim. Left unchecked, they rule us. The soul climbs higher, moved by values rooted in love for others, for truth, for something greater. Trials are a temptation to snap back, a hurdle blocking the noble path. Mindfulness equips us to meet them with poise, turning stumbles into strides. Each time we choose patience over rage and service over self, our moral spine strengthens. Temptations don't vanish, they just lose their volume, drowned out by a louder conscience.

Some people bounce around with no purpose. My own path bears this out. As a child I lived for acceptance and craved praise. High school was a parade of applause. I set records in track, basketball, and football. I enjoyed a pristine image as the kid who didn't drink or curse. Multiple colleges recruited me, and parents wanted me to date their daughters. I founded a Fellowship of Christian Athletes chapter and basked in the glow of approval. College at Duke shattered that. A small fish in a vast pond, I floundered. Girls weren't impressed, and neither were my coaches and professors. I partied to fit in, chasing acceptance, but I woke up hollow. When I reflected on my high school years, I realized what a hypocrite I'd been. I let my ego take over. I worked long hours to become physically strong and skilled. I was witty and quick to impress or intimidate others. I loved being successful and admired. But my selfish self was empty inside.

As mentioned earlier, after two years at college, disillusioned and feeling like a failure, I fled to the tip of West Virginia, where I hammered nails as a carpenter, bounced drunks at a bar, and drove to work in silence, radio off, wrestling with questions about who I was and what I wanted in life. The turning point came when I realized I'd been living a shallow existence and made the conscious decision that there would be no more aimless bouncing around.

Stripped of applause, I rebuilt. Values like integrity and purpose replaced ego. Back at Duke, over the next few years, that shift bore fruit: I stopped partying and went from near-flunking grades to being on the dean's list, becoming captain of the football team, and being drafted into the NFL by the New York Jets. But the real pivot came after college. I question whether the goal of becoming a millionaire by the age of thirty was really my true purpose. But it took me a while to figure it out. I didn't get the answer until I joined my church at age thirty-two and found purpose in seeking to find God's word through inspiration, revelation, and spiritual guidance instead of praise and financial riches.

Too often, our emotions dictate our actions and reactions, thrusting us toward choices we wouldn't otherwise make. I've learned to step back, observe my feelings with mindfulness, and then deliberately decide how I want to respond. There's a confidence and peace that comes from knowing which emotions I'll let pilot me and which values I'll hold fast to. Armed with this clarity, I feel ready to face life's daily struggles without fear. I know who I am, what I'll do, and that, in the end, things will work out for the best. They always do. A line from the Book of Mormon often helps me refocus when I stray. A prophet asks, "Why am I angry with my enemy?" It's a simple question that pulls me back to center.

On my ranch, I had two bulldozers, three tractors, and a massive brush cutter. I loved clearing fields and forests, carving out roads and lakes, and riding my motorcycle through towering cedar trees, splashing across streams, with the cool air rushing past me. It was exhilarating. Yet something felt incomplete. Despite the ranch improvements and turning a profit, I wasn't fulfilled. I hadn't yet figured out the root of my restlessness because I hadn't defined who I wanted to be or the values that would guide me. So I threw myself back into the mental grind of the business world.

I tackled all sorts of projects, pouring in long hours for tangible outcomes. I thrived on designing and completing real estate deals, building organizations, and taking on roles that fit my skills and experience. In hindsight, though, my motivations were narrow. I was driven to prove myself to my father. My focus zeroed in on the "doing." That meant surviving, creating, leading, competing, and growing financially and socially. I made friends (and a few enemies), but my energy went into action and achievement. Those particular "ings" consumed me, overshadowing a more important "ing," simply *being*. I should have prioritized projects that better reflected my values. If I'd focused more on people than on problems, my relationships—and my life, in general—would have been richer and more joyful.

PURPOSE FORGED IN THE FIRE OF TRIAL AND ERROR

My career was a saga of trial and error. I formed a venture capital company because I knew a lot of players in the industry. But most of them weren't eager to share their investments with me. I would tell people about potential deals, and they thanked me and sent me on my way. Lesson learned: Before you jump into a new business, gain a full appreciation of its complexities. I had capital, financial savvy, and operational experience, but I didn't have the staff to provide in-depth financial analysis, a network of M&A attorneys, and due diligence experts.

Through the VC, I sank four hundred thousand dollars into a TV station and lost it all. After that, I tried my hand at real estate. I bought land in Thornton, Colorado, and hired architects to design a 150-unit multifamily housing development and golf course. But by the time we'd whittled down the design to affordable rental rates, I didn't want my name on the mediocre project, so I sold it to a builder. I learned to be willing to shelve a project that doesn't live up to my values from this experience.

In search of a better niche, I invested in the creation of luxury units in Deer Valley, Utah. The location and development were ideal since there were already million-dollar condos and fine restaurants in the area. Without the appropriate experience, though, banks weren't inclined to give me a construction loan, so I put three million dollars of my own funds into building a high-end, ski-in/ski-out development, The Woods. In the mornings, before work, I'd take a few runs in the freshly groomed snow down to the lodge for breakfast. It was a beautiful way to live, but it didn't last.

By the time I finished my units, interest rates had skyrocketed to 18 percent, and President Jimmy Carter had eliminated tax deductions for owners of second homes and urged businesses and labor unions to limit wage increases to 7 percent annually.

And it turned out that the builder I hired was an alcoholic. Eventually, I was happy to sell the project at cost and recoup my personal investment while many other developers went bankrupt. Another lesson learned: For me, there was not much satisfaction in developing luxury condos for the rich and famous. I knew I needed to live a better life according to my purpose. What engagements would best use my values, talents, and resources? Building luxury dwellings was not it. I'd thought I was looking for an occupation I would enjoy, but more importantly, in reality, I was searching for the person I wanted to become.

Not long afterward, I received an offer to work in London's financial district. It seemed perfect. This is where it all happens, I thought. But after praying overnight, I asked myself if being a money changer was what I wanted. And I knew it wasn't. I wanted to better link my professional life with my purpose. If it didn't fit into that rubric, it wasn't worth doing.

What is meaningful—or purposeful—to another person, of course, might well be different. What my experience highlights is the importance of finding *your* purpose and connecting your actions with it, not to say what someone else's specific priorities should be. That is a question you must answer yourself. I arrived at the decision not to take the London job by taking the time to review the offer within the context of my values and purpose. It's the type of review that can be valuable for any endeavor you consider.

LESSONS LEARNED

From all these experiences, I have learned lessons that helped me better navigate my world.

- There is opposition in all things: good and evil, pleasure and pain, light and darkness, faith and fear.
- Trials, temptations, and challenges force us to either strengthen or abandon our values. Trials are "the refiner's fire." The bigger the trial, the greater the opportunity to further internalize your values.
- We must commit to acting on values rather than emotions. Hold to your values and not your sword.
- There is an ongoing battle for your soul. If you don't recognize that this is a war, you may be losing it.
- Seek to know the source of truth. Your Creator will not abandon you and will guide you but will not infringe on your freedom of choice.
- Anger does not lead to problem solving.

- Placing labels on people only hardens misunderstanding and lessens opportunities to align and work together.
- Everyone is gifted with a conscience, but guidance only comes from listening and acting accordingly.
- Blaming only fuels contention. Don't shift blame. No one can make you feel something, so state how *you* feel instead of suggesting that *they* make you feel a certain way.
- Listen attentively and be slow to offer your solution. Help another develop their own solution. If they develop and own the solution, they will work harder to implement it and not blame you if it doesn't work out.

TRACING BACK THE UNEASE

My friend Carl taught me something that's pure genius: Become a detective when you experience discomfort. When he'd feel vaguely bad, characterized by being overcome with sadness or unease without a clear reason for it, he'd rewind his days. Did he snap at someone? Brush off a plea for help? Sabotage someone's efforts? Once, after he traced his unease to a curt remark he'd made, unnoticed in the moment, guilt nudged him, and he apologized, vowing to watch his tongue. Decades of this activity honed his values into instincts, and regrets became rare.

Still, he told me that getting to that stage had been far from easy. "My parents were good people and raised me to be the same, to follow the Golden Rule and treat others with kindness and compassion," he said. "However, they didn't provide much in the way of structure or techniques for becoming such a person. They left that for me to figure out." He admitted that when he was younger, he was selfish and inconsiderate. He let his emotions take over, stirring impetuous and rude behavior.

Over time, he got serious about aligning acts with beliefs. Like a sculptor chiseling stone, he shaped himself through practice, shrugging off inevitable setbacks. To Carl's credit, he listened to his conscience and brought his behavior in line with his values. His method of reviewing his behavior by using emotional cues fits well with my message that we must work to harmonize our words, actions, beliefs, and deeds by internalizing our values.

This is true in the same way that concert pianists or other star performers don't simply rely on their natural talent to achieve success. They invest hours of practice over many years to perform at the highest level. Similarly, we must strive to get better at putting our values into action by recognizing key moments and reviewing our behavior. But we shouldn't get discouraged by setbacks. We can use the lessons we learn from challenges or trials to improve our ability to live our values and fulfill our purpose.

In my own life, I experienced a brutal day filled with numerous trials, a day like no other I'd endured. While sitting in my Salt Lake City condo, mulling over my attorney's advice to file for bankruptcy, my pregnant wife called from our ranch to report that seven feet of snow had fallen, and the buffalo had escaped. Then our doctor delivered the crushing recommendation to terminate our pregnancy, warning that our child had a dire prognosis and we'd be overwhelmed by medical expenses.

Overcome with despair, I knelt in prayer, and a question surfaced in my mind. "What is going right for you?" I answered that we had our health, our faith, and the assurance that our church's welfare system would prevent us from going hungry. The response came. "If you possess all that and still aren't content, your priorities are not in order." Rising from my knees, I felt renewed optimism and gratitude for my blessings.

A demonstration of the advantages of examining behavior at a collective level occurred just before the dawn of the twenty-first century when planeloads of Southern Baptists descended on Salt Lake City for their national gathering. To outsiders, the Southern Baptists and members of the Church of Jesus Christ of Latter-day Saints might appear to share similarities. Both were politically conservative, morally devout, and hungry for converts. Both denominations revered Jesus and denounced alcohol.

However, when discussions turned to doctrine, expressions of "I love you, brother" swiftly devolved into "You'll burn in hell, sister." LDS members grew resentful of the Southern Baptists' presence in Utah, perceiving their intent as an attempt to "save the saints." Our beloved prophet, President Hinckley, urged grace. He emphasized that the visitors meant well and deserved a warm reception. He taught that every faith holds some measure of truth, which we should embrace to improve ourselves. "Please refrain from being discourteous to these well-meaning individuals," he counseled.

This call for compassion and openness continues, and it encourages us to look beyond our own viewpoints, a practice that counters self-absorption and sharpens our self-awareness. By valuing the perspectives of others, we invite growth and move closer to our highest aspirations.

EXPANDING THE HORIZON

Self-absorption narrows our perspective to a mere speck, while concern for others expands it vastly. One effective method to keep our actions in line is to consider how others perceive them. What seems justifiable to us initially may appear less so from someone else's standpoint. This awareness extends to seeking divine guidance as well. Evaluating our conduct against a higher standard reveals areas where we fall short of the person we aim to be.

Shifting from self-focus to a broader outlook is a recurring theme across world religions. In Islam, submitting to God's will enables individuals to rise above their ego and selfish impulses. Buddhism teaches cultivating selflessness and compassion and performing acts of generosity and kindness. Similarly, Christianity emphasizes love, compassion, and service to others, epitomized in the command to love one's neighbor as oneself.

Growth emerges from adversity and struggle, not from ease and indulgence. Psychologists note that challenges trigger a fight or flight response, but there's a third, more constructive option: to rise above the situation by acting proactively rather than reactively. Base your actions on your principles, not fleeting emotions. Fight, flight, or make it right!

The ancient Stoics practiced a technique called the "view from above" to contextualize their difficulties. By stepping outside themselves, staying mindful, and viewing a situation from a broader perspective, they gained clarity. Imagine someone observing your location from thirty thousand feet. They wouldn't even see you. From another planet, only Earth itself is visible, not the life on the planet. To the Stoics, this showed that our troubles, however significant to us, fade into insignificance from a grand enough vantage point. This isn't to say we should ignore our problems or abandon our values but rather that we shouldn't let anxiety paralyze our ability to address them.

BECOMING OUR VALUES

Recently, I had an interesting talk with a young man who maintained he wanted to live according to righteous values and embrace the qualities that Jesus Christ exemplified, but pride prevented him from turning himself over to God. I told him he could not do it alone and discussed with him the need to lay his will upon the altar, to surrender to God's higher power as the route to achieving that kind of life. He saw the light.

Values are the building blocks of our character. Trials shape us. Each triumph sends out waves, uplifting others as it elevates us. Reflect on the past's teachings, embody today's decisions, and imagine tomorrow's self. The journey twists and turns. It is imperfect, human, uniquely ours. Through mindfulness, reflection, and faith, we change ideals into who we are, one intentional step at a time. And that takes time and perseverance.

9
Staying the Course

IMAGINE YOU'VE UNEARTHED YOUR LIFE'S purpose: to cultivate a way of being that resonates with your values, shaping you into the person you aspire to become. At first glance, it might seem like the hard part is over and that the path ahead will unfold effortlessly. But the truth is that bringing your life into harmony with your values is a marathon, not a sprint.

Becoming the fullest, truest version of yourself demands unwavering dedication, a commitment that stretches across decades. It's about weaving your principles so tightly into the fabric of your being that acting in harmony with them feels as natural as breathing. And yet, even after all that effort, perfection remains elusive. Missteps are inevitable.

This pursuit isn't a task you can check off a list and call done. There's no moment where you declare, "I've arrived," and coast through life, untouchable. We're human, not statues carved from marble. Errors will creep in, and that's not a flaw. It's a gift. Each sunrise offers a fresh chance to refine who we are and edge closer to our ideal selves. That's the quiet thrill of existence. As long as we draw breath, we can grow. There's no expiration date on becoming better.

I felt this truth not long ago in a moment I'm not proud of. My patient, kind wife made an innocent remark. Something had been simmering inside me, unaddressed and unnoticed. Before I could stop myself, I spoke harshly, ruining the peace of our evening. She didn't deserve my sharpness. The air grew heavy with my regret. But then came the repair: an apology, sincere and swift. In its wake, we both softened, lifted by the grace of reconciliation. It was a small but potent reminder that this journey of embodying our values is lifelong. We stumble, we mend, and in the mending, we rise.

Living your best life—staying true to your purpose—means affixing yourself to your values and letting them manage your actions, day after day. It's not hard to do this sporadically, and a single act of integrity might feel like a victory. But to weave those acts into a tapestry of virtue across a lifetime? That's the real challenge. It takes intention, resilience, and a willingness to keep going when the winds of circumstance blow against you. Trials, as we've explored, aren't obstacles to dread. They're the forge where our values are strengthened. Yet in those heated moments when stress overwhelms or emotions flare, our principles can blur. We're tempted to shove aside that quiet inner voice, our conscience, and react impulsively. Later, staring at the wreckage of our choices, we wonder why we didn't listen.

Emotions, situations, or the sway of others can hijack our behavior, pulling us off course. I've laid out tools to reclaim control and tether actions to values. Now we turn to the long game: how to sustain it through the years. The goal is to etch this practice so much into your mind that when life throws its curveballs, you either stand firm in your values instinctively or summon the strength to resist the pull of lesser impulses.

FOLLOWING THE COMPASS OF CONSCIENCE

At its heart, this journey is a tug-of-war between light and shadow, right and wrong. The clearer your values become, the stronger your moral compass grows and the more you can expect life to test it. Defining your purpose as living those values doesn't simplify the road. It illuminates it. Challenges don't vanish, they sharpen. That's where your conscience steps in to be a steady rudder through the storm. Some call it the Holy Spirit, others the soul's whisper or the echo of wisdom from enlightened minds. Whatever name it bears, it's universal. We all carry this inner beacon. Ignore it and its signal fades. Heed it and it becomes a trusted companion, lighting your way.

When we tune in to that voice, something remarkable happens: Our values don't just live on a checklist we consult in a crisis, they become part of us. Decisions flow not from deliberation but from instinct honed by practice. Choosing between that guiding voice and the clamor of immediate urges stops being a draining debate. It's simply who we are. Earlier, we talked about key moments, those flashes when emotions surge and the stakes feel high. These are the proving grounds. Instead of lashing out, pause. Rise above the fray. Meet the moment with grace, respect, and even love. It's not easy, but it's through these ordeals that our conscience can steer us true.

I've seen this in people who've walked this path longer than most. They don't glance backward, second-guessing their moral footing. Their eyes are forward, scanning for chances to lift others. Their values aren't a burden, they're a lens through which they see the world and move through it. That's the vision to chase: a life where your principles aren't just rules you follow but the heartbeat of who you've become.

A PERSONAL GUIDE

As a teenager, lost in the haze of youth, night after night, I'd kneel and recite prayers by rote. But the words felt hollow. Then, lying in bed, I'd conjure an image of myself at ninety, gazing down from the ceiling. I didn't want that old man to look back with regret, so I'd ask him for wisdom, for a nudge toward choices I'd be proud of at life's end. And every time, an answer came. At first, I thought this exercise was just good planning. Later, I recognized it as something more: a divine whisper, a guiding spirit meeting me in a form I could grasp. It taught me that this inner voice waits for us all, ready to speak if we seek and listen.

Your beliefs might frame it differently. Maybe it's God, the universe, or your own subconscious rising to the occasion. However you frame this personal guide, it grows stronger with a listening ear. Picturing the person you want to be sharpens your aim. It's like holding a mirror to your soul, reflecting not just who you are but who you could become. I've found strength in studying sacred texts and the words of great thinkers, but whatever your tradition, there's power in seeking wisdom beyond yourself.

PERSONAL VIRTUES IN ACTION

As I was wrapping up my real estate ventures, Rick Warner, a prominent Utah businessman and car-dealership magnate, approached me with an opportunity to invest in Alpnet, a technology company specializing in language translation software. I toured their offices. "I'm not too impressed with your management team," I later told him.

A few months later, he called me back. "I got rid of the management. I want you to run the company."

Initially, I turned down his proposal, but during prayerful consideration, I received unexpected advice. "If this is a good use of your talents and time, why don't you accept his offer?"

"Well, this is a risky venture," I replied, "and I don't want a failure on my record."

The insight that followed was, "You're more concerned about what people will think of you than about using your talents wisely. How does your thinking jibe with your values?"

I realized that running a company offering a valuable product was a worthy pursuit, so I accepted the role. The month I started, we hemorrhaged five hundred thousand dollars, but soon after, we secured deals with IBM and the CIA. Eventually, we took the company public, and our stock soared beyond my wildest dreams. During a talk with an investment group in New York when someone asked if the stock would keep climbing, I replied candidly, "I think it's already overvalued." Strangely, my honesty sparked speculation of some hidden strategy, fueling more purchases and pushing the price even higher.

Then IBM told us they planned to distribute our software for personal computers. I woke up in a cold sweat one night, realizing PC users weren't ready for our complex tool. "You shouldn't sell this software," I told my IBM contact.

"Why not?" he asked. "We've tested it and are using it ourselves. It's going to go gangbusters. It's amazing that you can translate back and forth from English to forty different languages. We want to sell it."

"Your users are computational linguists," I explained. "Put it on PC for the general public and you'll drown in customer complaints."

A few days later, he called back. "You're right. Thank you."

That decision tanked our business plan and frightened investors. But my commitment to the value and virtue of honesty held firm. I followed Gramps advice: "Just carry on, and it will work out." Soon we developed an even better plan, acquiring translation agencies in fourteen countries to create the world's first global translation network. Our software turbocharged translator productivity and precision, landing us contracts to translate manuals for giants like Ford, Apple, and WordPerfect, among others.

PASSING THE TORCH OF PURPOSE

We inherit *many* values from our parents, both noble and flawed. If we're fortunate and intentional, we refine those values and pass along the better ones to our children. Throughout my life, in both career and family, the greatest satisfaction has come from witnessing others strengthen their moral backbone. It's one thing to achieve success; it's another to do it with integrity.

What brings me the deepest reward is seeing my children, grandchildren, and colleagues live and lead with moral purpose. In 2022, one of my sons, Zach, became president of IndustryPro, the company I founded over thirty years earlier and which has orchestrated billions of dollars of business ownership transfers. But our true legacy isn't just measured in transactions. It's in the values we bring to every negotiation. As mentioned, we operate with transparency, clearly stating our terms and dealing honestly with buyers and sellers. This culture of integrity fosters a shared sense of purpose. It builds trust, and that trust empowers us to take bold risks, unleash creativity, and ultimately, deliver greater results.

What I've come to realize is this: Not only can individuals live with purpose, so can businesses. When an organization is grounded in principles and driven by a moral compass, it becomes more than a company. It becomes a force for good. Zach skipped my years of aimlessness and will become a far better leader than I was. (And despite family tradition, I doubt I'll ever fire him.) With pride and gratitude I can say my daughters and other son enjoy successful careers that are magnified by their righteousness.

RESPONSIBILITY AND FREEDOM OF CHOICE

Listening to the quiet whisper of our spirit honors our freedom to choose. We often rely on emotions, inspiration, or intuition, but to live a purposeful life, we must go further. We should seek and heed the guidance of our conscience, or those subtle nudges will fade, leaving us adrift without a moral anchor. Though we're born with a conscience, we must actively listen and take responsibility for shaping the values that direct us.

In the summer of 1976, I fell seriously ill on a business trip, around the time Legionnaires' disease was making headlines. With the medical community on high alert for this mysterious disease, an Atlanta hospital refused to admit me and sent me home. My condition worsened on the flight, and I was carried off the plane on a stretcher. A second hospital, this time in Denver, refused to admit me suggesting I go home and "sleep it off." Back in Spokane, I entered the local hospital. Doctors suspected Rocky Mountain Spotted Fever, but confirmation would take weeks, and I was desperately ill. My sister-in-law, a physician, encouraged them to try tetracycline. "We'll give it a shot," they said. "Otherwise, he'll be dead by tomorrow." My fever broke, and I pulled through, though I lost significant weight.

As I recovered, my mother asked, "Has this changed you at all?"

"What do you mean?" I replied.

"Has it shifted how you see things?" She was curious if my brush with death had reshaped my view on life.

I said no. This was years before my awakening. I was too unaware and caught in the moment to reflect. I could have asked myself what the purpose of life is, but I didn't. Had I grappled with it then, I might have found wisdom sooner. My world was small, centered on sports, recognition, business success, and living in a Duty/Justice mindset. Now my perspective has broadened. I notice the emotions behind people's faces. I'm curious about understanding others, dedicated to serving, and open to looking beyond myself. That shift has enriched my life immensely.

Adopting a Love/Trust approach expands your world by lowering walls. Free from self-absorption, your vision sharpens, letting you truly see others, value their perspectives, and connect with compassion instead of fear or tallying points. Some people naturally live this way. For me, it took effort. Now I share these insights at work with young employees, fresh from school, engaging with business owners. These owners, often strapped for time, may challenge or test others to gauge trustworthiness. I lead my team to face these moments with kindness, not aggression, and with compassion and confidence.

In pivotal moments, I ask myself if I'm improving a situation or making it worse. Am I letting trivial matters overshadow what's important? I've noticed that most natural Love/Trust individuals were raised in homes that nurtured those qualities. But many of us, even from good families, must learn this ourselves. The effort pays off. Don't give up or assume it's beyond you. Don't delay becoming the person you're capable of being. Commit to patience, even loving those who oppose you, and rewards will follow.

As mentioned earlier, properly assigning responsibility ties into self-awareness, a principle I emphasize to my kids and colleagues. It's about living in the present, not trapped in the past, accepting a situation rather than pointing fingers, and then acting to improve it.

Recently, Zach, told me that when he'd been a business consultant, he'd used one of my lessons on placing responsibility in his work with a client who stored custom furniture for interior designers. Salespeople were wasting time hunting for parts in the warehouse because the staff wouldn't tag them with RFID (radio frequency identification) codes. My son told the warehouse staff their job was to support the sales force, and the sales force would decide if they warranted a bonus. That's placing responsibility where it belongs. The warehouse staff hadn't realized who they were serving, but soon, their performance improved. In business, we must know our customers. In life, we must understand our purpose.

Even now, on slow days I catch myself wondering if I will feel productive. It's wise to regularly assess where we stand and what we're contributing. My morning prayer consists of me telling the Heavenly Father, "This is what I want to accomplish today, but your will be done." Knowing he's listening pushes me to set laudable goals and feel accountable. At night, I reflect on how I did. I tell young people, "There's a war going on for your soul. If you're not checking in with your Commander-in-Chief about how you can make a difference in this war, you might be losing it."

One time, I let my frustration over things not going as planned override my better judgment, and I lashed out in a way I later regretted. It happened while I was managing thirteen acquisitions for Alpnet. Our strategy was to integrate our software into these newly acquired companies, boosting their accuracy and efficiency.

It was the early days of digital data transmission when sending files over phone lines between countries was becoming practical. A country like Switzerland, for example, taxed us for bringing in a hard drive but charged nothing if we transmitted the data remotely. This technological shift influenced our decision to acquire translation bureaus globally. At the time, we served major clients like Apple, General Motors, Rolls-Royce, Ford, and other big names in the automotive industry. Our headquarters were in Utah, but I was based in England. Years earlier, I had hired Walt Mogan as VP of Marketing, and by this point, I suspected he had his sights set on becoming CEO. Walt also oversaw sales, and with a worldwide company retreat approaching, I needed to review his new remuneration and commissions schedule for each country before presenting it at the conference.

"Where's the plan, Walt?" I asked repeatedly. "I need to approve it before we present it at the conference."

He'd reply, "Oh, I'll get it to you." But it never arrived. I was truly frustrated.

Meanwhile, he invited the key employee of our major shareholder to the retreat—supposedly just to observe—while we were still navigating the chaos of the acquisitions and our recent move to go public. When Walt finally began to unveil his remuneration schedule at the retreat, I seethed with frustration and cut him off. "Okay, Walt. Stop there. We haven't reviewed this. You're totally out of order. We're not going to do this right now." I was visibly upset. The room went silent. It felt like my days as a bouncer, when a fight would break out, shattering the good vibes, and it'd take twenty minutes for the energy to recover. The outburst drained all the goodwill from the meeting.

Elizabeth, our country manager in France, called me out. "Fred, you're always telling us to work together, but you're not setting a very good example."

She was right.

I could have tackled it better by softening my response, saying it was Walt's preliminary plan and we needed to discuss it. Later, I realized Walt had set me up. He had survived the politics of a huge company and was using his skill against me. By inviting the shareholder's right-hand man to witness the scene, he ensured I would be painted in a bad light. That observer left the retreat, reported to the board that I was a hothead, and said they should let me go if I wanted to leave.

Looking back, I see how my lack of emotional control cost me. If I'd been more attuned to the impact of my actions and kept my temper in check, I could have handled it differently. At that moment, Alpnet had the potential to become the world's foremost translation bureau. We'd pioneered innovative approaches, but after I left, the company lost momentum, customers drifted away, and the business gradually faded.

Walt should have submitted the plan to me prior to the conference, but rather than repeatedly demanding the plan and losing my cool when he stalled, here's how I could have approached it more effectively.

1. **Find a good time to talk:** "Walt, I'm in Europe and you're in Utah. When's a good time for us to sync up?"

2. **Confirm the relationship:** "You bring a wealth of experience to Alpnet, Walt. Your work is making a real impact, and I appreciate your contributions."

3. **Voice the issue:** "Our world conference is coming up fast, and we need to unveil the commission plan. I'm frustrated because I haven't seen it yet. Are you holding off on sharing it with me?"

4. **Recognize the other person's perspective:** "You're the best qualified to draw up the commission plan. Do you have a problem with me reviewing it?"

5. **Invite a solution:** "Think it over and let me know tomorrow when you can get me the full plan for my review. We need ample time before the conference."

6. **Share resolution if/when you get it:** "Great! So we're set. You commit to delivering it to me next week, at least five days before the event."

This approach could have kept things collaborative, avoided the public clash, and preserved the team's momentum—maybe even the company's future. If only I'd exercised the virtues I've since embraced, my life would have unfolded differently.

SUSTAINING VIRTUES

Virtues are not trophies you win once and display on a shelf, gleaming and untarnished forever. They're more like gardens: carefully planted, diligently tended, and always at risk of being overtaken by weeds if neglected. We spend years nurturing these traits, but the work doesn't end when they take root. Life has a way of testing our resolve by throwing storms of stress, temptation, or apathy our way. How do we keep those virtues alive and thriving? How do we avoid slipping back into old habits or letting them erode under pressure? Following are some practical strategies to safeguard what you've built.

DAILY RITUALS

Virtues thrive on steady practice, not one-off dramatic acts. Build simple, deliberate habits to uphold your values daily. For kindness, begin each day with a quiet resolve. "Today, I'll find ways to share a warm word or gesture." For integrity, take a moment before choices, big or small, to reflect on whether the choice you're considering is true to who you aim to be. These practices don't need to be grand. A quick note of gratitude in a notebook or a mindful pause to gather patience before reacting can suffice. With time, these small acts weave into your character, anchoring you firmly when life's storms arise.

BUILD A FORTRESS OF AWARENESS

Falling back into bad habits often begins in those moments when you're too distracted, stressed, or tired to notice old patterns creeping in. Self-awareness is your watchtower. Train yourself to spot the early warning signs: a sharper tone creeping into your voice (like the way I talked to my wife), a flicker of envy dimming your generosity, a shortcut luring you away from honesty. Keep a mental log or even jot down reflections at day's end. What tested me today? Where did I shine? Where did I waver? This isn't about self-criticism, it's about illumination. When you see the cracks forming, you can shore them up before they widen into chasms.

Every virtue has its kryptonite—specific situations or emotions that loosen your grip on it. Maybe impatience flares when you're rushed, or generosity falters when you feel unappreciated. Identify these tripwires. Sketch them out. "When X happens, I tend to Y." Then plan your countermeasures. If stress makes you curt, practice a five-second pause before speaking. If pride tempts you to bend the truth, rehearse a humble fallback. "I don't know, but I'll find out." Awareness includes knowing your weak spots. And that makes you strategic.

As I've aged, I've also begun reflecting each evening on how I've served others that day by asking, "Who did I help?" I admire those who start their day wondering who they can serve that day. I use small markers to gauge my progress. The first step is connecting with people. That can be as simple as chatting with cashiers, neighbors, or anyone nearby. These interactions reveal ways we can help, and the interactions themselves may help the person with whom we're connecting feel better about their day. We can volunteer with organizations, but it's just as vital to notice those around us. Just asking simple questions may be enough. Asking someone how their day is going can open the door to understanding their life, their challenges, and what's important to them. And it may also inspire you. For example, someone might share they're volunteering at a hospital, sparking your own interest in doing some kind of volunteer work.

This approach works in professional settings too. "What are your priorities? Your biggest challenges?" I ask colleagues. "How can I help?" Making these questions a habit at work naturally extends to life beyond it. Asking and listening is far more engaging than talking about myself. It's how I learn. If I can't recall moments of service in my day, it's a sign my world is shrinking, focused only on me. Happiness grows with the size of our world, and service is the key to expanding it.

PACE YOURSELF FOR THE LONG HAUL

Burnout is a silent thief, sapping the energy you need to live virtuously. If you're exhausted—physically, emotionally, spiritually—your resolve weakens, and old vices whisper louder. Guard against this by pacing yourself. Step away, meditate, breathe in nature—whatever refills your well. Virtue isn't relentless perfection, it's sustainable growth.

SURROUND YOURSELF WITH MIRRORS AND PILLARS

Seek out friends, mentors, or even strangers whose actions inspire you and who reflect your virtues back to you. They're mirrors, showing you what's possible, and pillars, holding you steady when you sway. If you've worked to cultivate humility, spend time with someone who listens more than they speak. If resilience is your prize, seek out those who've weathered their own storms with grace. Distance yourself from influences that pull you backward, including cynics who mock your patience and manipulators who prey on your trust. Your virtues don't exist in a vacuum. They're nourished or starved by the company you keep.

FORGIVE YOURSELF AND GO FORWARD

You will falter. A promise will bend and a selfish impulse will win out. It's not a question of if, but when.

When you falter, your mind can spin a harsh tale, telling you you're weak or you'll never change. Don't let that narrative stick. Reframe it as a chapter, not the book. "I snapped today, but I caught it faster than last time," or "I hesitated to help, but I still did." By recasting setbacks as progress, you rob them of their power to drag you backward.

The danger isn't in the stumble, it's in letting that stumble define you. Instead of spiraling into guilt or despair, forgive yourself with purpose. Acknowledge the slip. Acknowledge that you've veered off course, and then pivot, asking yourself what you can do to realign. Maybe it's an apology, a quiet recommitment, or a step to make amends. Each act of self-forgiveness builds a bridge back to your virtues, keeping you from sinking into the quicksand of old habits.

REVISIT YOUR WHY

Virtues can fade when they lose their meaning. Periodically step back and reconnect with why you chose these qualities in the first place. Why did courage matter so much you fought to claim it? What drew you to compassion over indifference? Write it down, speak it aloud, or picture the person you'd be without them. Maybe honesty became your core because you saw the wreckage of deceit in someone else's life. Maybe gratitude lifted you out of bitterness once, and you swore never to forget it. This *why* is your compass. When you feel it slipping from your grasp, hold it close. It will take you back.

CELEBRATE THE QUIET VICTORIES

It's easy to overlook the moments when you *don't* fall back, when you resist making a cruel retort, stand firm in a tough choice, or extend kindness where it's undeserved. These aren't fireworks worthy triumphs, but they're the bricks of your character. Pause to honor them. Whisper to yourself, "I did that." Recognizing when you've held the line reinforces your commitment, making it harder to retreat next time.

RELY ON A HIGHER VISION

Sometimes, maintaining virtue feels bigger than you, and maybe it is. Whether you draw strength from faith, an appreciation for legacy, or a belief in something transcendent, tether your efforts to a larger purpose or exemplar. Imagine the ripple effect: your patience calming a room, your honesty inspiring trust, your perseverance lighting a path for others. Or as I did in earlier years, picture facing your older self as you approach the end of your time on this earth, proud of the person you've stayed true to. This vision lifts you beyond the daily grind, taking virtue from a task to a calling.

Tie your virtues to something bigger than the moment, a vision of what they'll leave behind. Picture your kindness echoing through the lives of your children and grandchildren. See your integrity molding a workplace long after you've gone. When you see your virtues as seeds for a future you may never witness, letting them slip feels weightier and staying on course feels uplifting.

TEST THEM IN SILENCE

Sometimes the loudest threats to virtue are the ones no one sees: private thoughts, unspoken grudges, quiet envies. Audit these shadows. Sit alone and ask yourself if you're harboring something that undermines what you've built. For the virtue of forgiveness, root out the bitterness you've buried. For gratitude, chase away the complaints that murmur in your head. Winning these inner battles matters because they're the undercurrent that either lifts your virtues or drags them down. Use low-stakes moments as training grounds to practice virtues. Stuck in traffic? Build patience by letting someone merge ahead.

As Christmas approached, I could not find a $270 jewelry item I bought for my wife. I called Amazon and told them I wasn't sure I'd received the package. I may have hidden it away and couldn't find it. They told me they'd send a replacement piece of jewelry. "But what if I find it later?" I asked.

"Simply return it," they replied.

A month later, I found the package and without hesitation sent it back. Looking back, that act further solidified my value of honesty. These micro-acts are like rehearsals. Each one tunes your instincts, so when the big tests come, your virtues aren't rusty.

WRAPPING IT UP

Growth comes from recognizing past missteps, learning from them, and committing to better decisions moving forward. I've had my share of regrets. As a boss, I've been intimidating, mishandled situations, and hurt people. I've since sought out those I wronged, apologized, and vowed to improve. Living your values in pivotal moments is essential to becoming the person you aspire to be.

Listening, discussing respectfully, and cocreating solutions work to everyone's benefit because they signal value, treating others as partners, not pawns. These skills can lift you from reactive, low-level behavior like anger or fear toward a higher state of love and trust.

Self-forgiveness is vital when you fall short. If our Creator pardons our efforts to grow, why can't we? Simultaneously, strive to rise above fear and resentment, aiming for trust and love. Or at least keep a clear vision of who you want to become. That mental image acts as a compass. When your actions stray, it guides you back. From your values and purpose, craft a vivid picture of your ideal self. In key moments, when there's a disconnect, rely on that vision to realign.

You don't drift into virtue, and you don't drift into keeping it. It's a choice, renewed daily, to live as the person you've fought to become. The road won't always be smooth, but with the tools I've outlined, you can walk it with your head high. That's not just holding on but pressing forward. A life of virtue isn't about never falling. It's about always rising. And it's a life brimming with examples that will be your legacy.

10

Purposeful Posterity

ONE GUSTY AFTERNOON, I PUSHED my kayak onto the lake's turbulent waters, eager for exercise despite the gathering storm clouds. As the wind intensified, churning the water into rough waves that splashed coldly against my face, I turned toward home. Fixing my gaze on the faint outline of my house across the lake, I paddled against relentless waves. As exhaustion crept into my muscles, a flicker of curiosity arose. What if I let the winds guide me? Setting my paddle down, I leaned back in the kayak, closed my eyes, and let the lake's currents and the gusts of wind steer my path.

Twenty minutes later, the kayak settled into a gentle sway, shielded from the howling winds. I opened my eyes, eager to see where fate had delivered me. To my dismay, I was in a secluded cove, surrounded by a flotilla of discarded plastic bottles, tangled fishing line, and other flotsam and jetsam. While I always carried a bag with me to collect floating cans and plastic bottles, this was too big a task, so I decided to leave it for the lake caretaker's weekly cleanup. Resolute, I threw my whole weight into paddling my journey homeward.

The wind and waves fought back, pushing me off course each time I paused to rest, but through dogged perseverance, I finally reached shore. After a hot shower warmed my chilled bones, I sat by the window, watching the storm's fury lash the lake. The ordeal etched a lesson into my mind: Drifting through life's storms without firm values throws us to like-minded, directionless company. A creditable journey demands a clear destination, steadfast effort, and the courage to press forward against resistance.

This experience on the lake opens a window to weightier questions: Where are you steering your life? What fuels the fire of your purpose? How will you pilot through the inevitable squalls to reach your goals? Equally vital is the legacy we leave for those who come after us—what I call *purposeful posterity*. Living with intention not only establishes our own path but also lights a signal for our children, grandchildren, and beyond, guiding them toward lives imbued with meaning and integrity. Purposeful posterity not only concerns personal fulfillment but also planting seeds of values and wisdom that will flourish in future generations.

Drawing from almost eight decades of life on this earth, I've distilled strategies for crafting a purposeful existence. They're not rigid prescriptions but flexible guideposts, adaptable to the unique contours of *your* journey. While our paths may diverge, the destination remains shared: to live deliberately, to grow into the fullest expression of ourselves, and to cultivate fulfillment, connection, and self-awareness. Purpose is not a static achievement but a dynamic process, one that evolves with each choice, challenge, and reflection.

BEYOND WORLDLY GOALS

Across spiritual traditions (Christian, Hindu, Muslim, Buddhist, and others), there is a common thread: Our actions in this life establish what lies beyond. Earthly existence is a crucible for growth. It's a place to learn, evolve, and refine our character. Material wealth and accolades, while seductive, often fade in significance compared to the enduring richness of relationships and personal integrity.

I made this point on a flight to China, a few years ago, when I sat next to Angelo, a young man from Hong Kong, raised by a mother who worked tirelessly at multiple jobs after his sailor father abandoned them. Despite these challenging early circumstances—or perhaps because of them—Angelo was full of life, brimming with curiosity, and quick to ask questions. His excitement about life and his future was infectious.

"What do you think the purpose of life is?" I asked, curious to learn more about this impressive young man.

"To make a living," he replied.

Given his precarious upbringing, his response was understandable. He craved a house, a car, and financial comfort. Many people prioritize earnings over purpose, often for seemingly good reasons like securing comfort that was once out of reach and enjoying the pleasures of this life with loved ones. But I pressed him, asking if wealth or renown alone could fulfill us. Apart from wealth and renown, what other purpose could you have on this earth? Although Angelo seemed ahead of where I was at his age, he didn't have a satisfactory answer, and our conversation moved on to other topics. I hope his purpose grew as mine eventually did.

My father's final months brought life's purpose into sharp focus. Confined to a recliner, blind and frail, he might have felt his life had dwindled to insignificance. But he embraced reflection, sifting through his experiences to share wisdom with us. Each labored breath seemed to affirm his core self, secured in values he believed were eternal: love, family, and faith. When he passed, a gentle smile lingered on his face, a quiet testament to a life well lived, measured in the end not by worldly triumphs but by the man he had become and the family he held dear.

This yearning for meaning appears woven into the human spirit. A 2025 Pew Research study found that 86 percent of American adults believe people have a soul or spirit in addition to their physical body, 83 percent believe in God or a universal spirit, 79 percent believe there is something spiritual beyond the natural world, and 74 percent believe in heaven, hell, or both.

We are much more than our physical bodies, something I didn't realize in my youth. As I've discussed, in my high school years, I was focused on my physical shell, my identity wrapped up in the speed, strength, and athleticism of my body. I measured my physical shell by outward appearance, races won, and victories scored. Most of my time was spent in "shell time," working out, getting ample sleep, eating, practicing, strategizing, and reviewing past contests. It was a shallow existence. I came to realize that being shell-centered made me self-centered while spiritual nourishment such as prayer, scriptures, meditating, and serving others was of greater consequence.

At the end of our days, we must be prepared to face our Creator and account for the lives we've led—the existence he granted us in this world—marrying our actions with the principles that define us. For me, this means striving to live in a way that honors my faith, my family, the pursuit of truth, and my commitment to growth, believing my efforts will resonate in this life and beyond.

I do this in the knowledge that there's a pervasive force of darkness that seeks to undermine light, truth, and meaning. This force, often subtle yet insidious, manifests in myriad forms: despair, deception, lust, contention, or the erosion of values that uplift the human spirit. It thrives in apathy, distraction, and the chaos of modern life, pulling individuals away from their higher calling and purpose. To live with intention and create a life in keeping with truth and goodness, we must first acknowledge we are engaged in a silent yet relentless battle, one that demands our awareness, courage, and resolve.

Recognizing this war is only the beginning. A purposeful life requires active resistance against the pull of negativity and falsehood. It calls for cultivating inner light through practices like prayer, mindfulness, gratitude, and integrity. To live purposefully is to stand as a warrior in this unseen war, armed with purpose and fortified by the conviction that even small, intentional acts can shift the balance away from darkness and toward light.

FAMILY: THE HEARTBEAT OF PURPOSE

For me, family stands as the cornerstone of purpose. They are a source of love, growth, and service. When my first child was born, I realized that to be the parent they deserved, I needed to grow up and set aside my selfishness for more commendable behavior. It was a major shift, and it didn't happen instantly. It unfolded over years of trial and error, but it grounded me in a truth that continues to influence me: Purpose flows from aligning our actions with the people and principles we hold dear.

Family profoundly influences who we are—physically, emotionally, mentally, and spiritually—weaving a complex legacy that defines our identity and values. I often find myself reflecting on the four living generations in my family, each contributing unique strengths, perspectives, and lessons that bind us together. I've also traced nine generations back, uncovering stories of resilience, sacrifice, and growth that continue to influence me. Each ancestor's life, with its triumphs and struggles, adds depth to our collective narrative, reinforcing the enduring power of familial bonds.

Recent losses—my three siblings' spouses—have drawn siblings closer, reminding us of the fragility and preciousness of our bonds. Together, we carry forward a legacy of service. My brother, Lew Jr., founded SIGN Fracture Care International, and it has restored mobility to over five hundred thousand people through medical training and free surgical supplies. My sister Ellen writes community histories and brings joy to memory-care residents with her storytelling. My sister Irene continues to counsel, offering wisdom to those in need. Our annual family reunions, cherished by my kids and grandchildren, weave cousins into lifelong allies, their laughter and shared adventures a testament to the enduring power of family.

As a parent, I carry a lingering regret: I wasn't always the safe haven my children needed to share their most intimate feelings. Work often consumed me, and I fell short as a compassionate listener. I've corrected this, but those early years remain a poignant lesson. My father often said, "If you were honest and sincere, all will work out." Those words proved to be prophetic. Today, my children are loving parents, showering our family with affection and binding us through shared values and faith. My wife, my partner, is a daily reminder of grace, filling my life with gratitude and grounding me in love.

Retirement thrust my father and me into an unexpected reckoning. Corporate upheaval had forced us both out of our careers, leaving us to nurse wounds in silence. For months we barely spoke, each grappling with the loss of identities tied to work. Then my mother's cancer diagnosis—six months to live—changed everything. In her final days, she urged us to reconcile, her voice soft but resolute. "I hope you and your dad can get back together." Her words lingered, a promise we both felt bound to keep. After her passing, we began meeting for lunches, tentative at first, the silences heavy with unspoken regrets. Over time, the warmth returned. Dad was not a hugger, but at age seventy-five, he received his first hug from me since my childhood. Soon the stiff, awkward feeling disappeared, and we often hugged long and hard. Work faded from Dad's mind, replaced by family—his True North—and Mom's absence taught me, too, that family eclipses all else.

Being fired by my Dad was a bitter pill, but it reshaped me. It taught me to view setbacks as lessons, not endpoints. I emerged sharper, more resilient, my perspective recast. My father's life, defined by his generation's breadwinner ethos, delayed his own reckoning with purpose. He poured himself into providing, only to discover, in his final years, that becoming his best self mattered more. His last smile, as his lungs gave out, wasn't just courage. It was certainty, a quiet assurance of a purposeful beyond. Even though he was drowning as his lungs filled with liquid, Dad shared that big smile, lovingly wanting his last breath to be a gift to us. Our journey—estrangement, loss, reunion—yielded clarity for me. Family outshines ambition. Work alone cannot fulfill us. Our purpose lies in becoming, not merely doing.

PARENTING (AND GRANDPARENTING) WITH INTENTION

My parents rarely spoke explicitly about values, but their actions taught us honesty, humility, and perseverance. A stern rebuke for arrogance or a quiet reminder to be honest shaped us more than any discussion about values could have. But mostly my siblings and I learned by watching and following their example. As a parent, I tried to do better, but I could have done more. Luckily, my children's religious education placed values at the forefront, and playful moments with my daughter Vivie—role-playing scenarios to overcome hurtful words—helped her grasp compassion early. At four, when I role-played rudeness, she said, "I don't feel good when I hear those things. Can we talk in a different way?" Those exchanges were seeds, planting empathy and resilience.

As a grandfather of nineteen kids, I'm more deliberate, seizing opportunities to have an impact through dialogue, not lectures. When my grandson William was an eighth-grader, he asked how to befriend new classmates who lingered awkwardly on the sidelines. I praised his compassion and offered practical tips: Ask open-ended questions, share a story, listen without judgment.

When I saw my granddaughter Kate baking cookies for a sick friend, I asked her to name the value she was living.

"Kindness," she replied.

I encouraged her to reflect on how it felt.

As twelve-year-old Jackson prepared breakfast, I posed a lighthearted question. "What's more important, compassion or breakfast?"

"Compassion," he replied. "But breakfast is important too." That sparked laughter, which was followed by a more serious conversation.

When young Caleb proudly discussed his savings, I commended his discipline but prompted him to consider a moral dilemma. Would he sell a faulty bike without telling the buyer it needed repairs?

These discussions, rooted in curiosity and affirmation, help my grandchildren associate their actions with purposeful values.

We must talk to our children and grandchildren about values explicitly, following up with supportive, nonjudgmental conversations. Encourage them to define their principles early and assess whether their actions match their ideals. Help them reflect on difficult moments. What could have been handled better? What lessons emerged? These dialogues build self-awareness and resilience, equipping them to face life's complexities with purpose.

The greatest joy comes from seeing loved ones hold on to righteous values and work through challenges. Our Creator certainly knows that feeling. For instance, I often told my kids that screening potential mates through a values filter would help avoid heartbreaking experiences. "You will marry someone who holds the same values you do, so act like the person you want to marry."

11

Creating a Purposeful Life

AT THE BEGINNING OF THIS book, I said that life has a way of opening your eyes and the things I was going to share came from my own experience. Honesty is one of my values, so you can count on the fact that I've been as honest and straightforward as possible in what I've imparted. I didn't come to the understandings I've unfolded here quickly or without moments of pain, embarrassment, and regret. But the reward has been a purposeful life. And maybe my experiences and what I've learned will help you get there too. We all have to find our own way, and none of us make the journey alone. For me and many others, the path to finding my own way has been made easier through my relationship with my Creator and with the help of wise advisors. I encourage you to nurture relationships that help you on your own way to a fulfilling life.

Fulfillment flows from purpose, and excavating our values begins the process because values serve as a compass, guiding us through both the turbulence and tranquility of life. Anchored values are a vital force that can provide clarity when we ask the important questions in life: Why am I here? What is most meaningful in my life? When we answer those question through the lens of our values, our spirits are uplifted and we feel connected with something greater than ourselves. Anchored values also sharpen our decision-making process because they provide the True North that guides us to a purposeful life.

Purpose strengthens both mind and body, easing stress and fostering habits that extend vitality and years. It begins with core values—what in our life is worth defending. Living those truths daily shapes a truer self. Purpose is uncovered through reflection and resolve, transforming life from surface skimming to profound depths, every step alive with meaning.

The foundation of a purposeful life lies in knowing what anchors you. What values stir meaning in your soul? Naming your values is the first step toward embodying them. Next, envision the person you aspire to become. How do these values manifest in your daily life, from the smallest gestures to the most significant decisions? Then take an honest inventory of your actions. Reflect on how you have acted throughout the day, consistently over time. Do they reflect your values or do they betray them? Do they spark joy and purpose or leave you feeling unmoored? If you find yourself off course, embrace the freedom to adjust. Shift your mindset, tweak your habits, or seek guidance to parallel your ideals. Values are not abstract ideals but living commitments, expressed through the choices you make each day.

And the choices we make every day do matter. Living our values is not a sporadic endeavor but a daily practice, a pursuit of consistency rather than perfection. Purposeful lives are built from purposeful days, each one a chance to inch closer to your aspirations. To stay focused, I begin each morning by creating a list of goals and activities. These then become a roadmap that provides clear awareness and structure. On days when I fall short, I resist the urge to dwell on failure. I don't beat myself up. I express gratitude for the gift of the day itself and resolve to do better tomorrow. Evening prayer serves as a quiet underpinning, offering affirmation and perspective. This rhythm of intention, action, and reflection makes the ordinary meaningful and weaves purpose into the fabric of daily life.

One thing that has helped me along the way has been the Three Levels of Awareness model. Like everyone, I've witnessed myself thinking and behaving from all three levels of awareness: Fear/Anxiety, Duty/Justice, and Love/Trust. In this model, the highest level, Love/Trust, represents the apex of personal growth. It marks a shift from *doing* to *being*, from self-centered priorities to a commitment to the well-being of others. At this level, compassion, empathy, and authenticity define our interactions, and trust in ourselves and others forms the bedrock of meaningful relationships. Love/Trust is a state of openness, where fear and ego yield to vulnerability and mutual respect. Those who embody this level radiate positivity, inspiring kindness and understanding in their communities.

Like many, I've navigated the full spectrum of awareness, from moments of struggle to glimpses of clarity. Each day, I strive to keep my thoughts, actions, and intentions in line with Love/Trust, recognizing it as a continuous journey. Living in this state enriches every facet of life. Personal fulfillment heightens, relationships flourish, and a sense of purpose becomes clear. By embracing Love/Trust, we unlock the potential to live with joy, create lasting bonds, and contribute meaningfully to the world, creating an influence that reaches far beyond our immediate circle. The Three Levels of Awareness model is always in the back of my head, quietly asking if I'm living by my values and making things better or on a downward spiral.

Of course, moving from Fear/Anxiety to Love/Trust requires learning and implementing a variety of skills. Accepting responsibility for one's actions, for instance, builds integrity and develops trust. Active listening, allowing others to feel heard, encourages collaboration, and boosts empathy. Problem-solving that is focused on solutions instead of blame addresses issues constructively and promotes teamwork. Remembering to commend others for their strengths uplifts both them and you, and when we acknowledge and compliment others for what they're doing with excellence, we strengthen our bonds with them.

Visualizing the desired self—the self that is living our values and is coming from a Love/Trust level of awareness—guides intentional actions, ensuring a life of purpose beyond mere achievements. These skills empower individuals to move from reactive behaviors to proactive, values-driven living.

Of course, transforming values into virtues requires sustained commitment, akin to an athlete's training. It involves visualizing virtuous behavior to prepare for real-life challenges, purposefully living values on a daily basis to build the muscles needed when life challenges us, and meeting trials and opposition with focus and intention, remembering that challenge is necessary to further strengthen and embed values into character, turning them into virtues over time.

Despite humanity's inclination toward peace, conflicts often arise from selfish desires overriding higher values. Everyone adheres to a set of beliefs, whether from religion, personal experiences, or societal norms, and exploring time-tested religious teachings can provide ethical clarity. Virtues such as compassion, humility, charity, and courage are values put into action, shaping a moral and meaningful life.

All of this work prepares us for key moments—major or minor decisions that test our principles under pressure. Key moments are critical junctures where emotions like anger or fear can cloud judgment. Recognizing them allows us to pause, reflect, and choose integrity over impulse, reinforcing our moral foundation.

Uncontrolled emotions can cloud judgment and derail progress toward goals, while intentional, collaborative choices foster habits, strengthen relationships, and build mutual respect. Virtues develop through consistent practice, reinforced by navigating challenges with clarity and purpose. Principled actions shape character and encourage trust, promoting ethical behavior within communities. In critical moments, I no longer react impulsively but approach decisions with calm confidence. When others are involved, I seek solutions that honor shared goals, working together to achieve outcomes that benefit all parties.

Not only do we all need considerable practice to get to this point, we need self-reflection because without it, honing our skills and ensuring that we are living our values on a consistent basis won't happen. This disciplined habit of stepping back from daily demands to evaluate our values, actions, and authenticity is essential for a meaningful life. It anchors us to our purpose, ensuring our choices align with our aspirations. In a world obsessed with recognition, self-reflection demands courage to confront flaws and grow. Tools like mindfulness, external perspectives, and lessons from successes and failures help refine our behavior.

Values transform into virtues through consistent practice and reflection, akin to mastering a craft over decades. This ongoing process nurtures personal growth and inspires others, creating a life of integrity and purpose.

I've lived most of my years already, and I'm not blind to my flaws. I've faltered, squandered opportunities, had moments of selfishness, and at times, drifted without direction. Yet that aimless younger self ignited a lifelong search for clarity, a quest that continues to shape me. With the years I have left, I aim to make a difference, to live in a way that honors my faith and my family. One day, I hope to stand before my Creator and hear, "Well done." My children, compassionate and wise beyond my early stumbles, are my guiding lights. As my body slows—joints stiffening, heart faltering—my resolve strengthens, buoyed by faith and a trust that trials are part of a divine plan.

By embracing values that lead to a purposeful life, I grow personally and hope to leave a legacy worth following. My aim is to live and think in the likeness of my Savior, Jesus Christ, ensuring my life's vocation carries forward, inspiring others to seek purpose, cherish relationships, and grow through every storm.

In sharing my journey, my deepest wish is for you to discover your own path to a purposeful life. May you uncover the values that anchor your soul, guide your decisions, and bring meaning to each day. I hope you find strength in reflection, courage in challenges, and joy in relationships that uplift and inspire. Let your values shape your virtues, and may your purposeful days build a life that not only fulfills you but also encourages others to seek their own paths with clarity and heart.

Acknowledgments

I THANK MY PARENTS, ALONG with the other truth seekers who clarified ageless principles that gave meaning and purpose to my life.

The Human Values Institute, led by C. Kay Allen and Roger K. Allen, provided the awareness and skills to align my actions with beliefs. Thank you.

In creating this book, my family, especially my daughter Alexandra, provided valuable feedback, while Malcolm Nicholl brought my words to life.

Ultimately, I must acknowledge my revered Creator, the source of all truth, whose purpose is to lead us to become like him and ultimately live together eternally.

About the Author

FRED ZIRKLE built a company that has bought and sold businesses valued in the billions of dollars in thirteen countries. He has served as president and CEO of both privately held companies and publicly traded firms including Key Tronic Corp., a computer hardware firm with $180 million in annual revenues, Alpnet, Inc., a computer software/services company with offices in twelve countries, and VentureSum, a venture capital organization. He serves as chairman of investment banking firm IndustryPro, which he founded more than thirty years ago.

Fred has been quoted in The *Wall Street Journal*, *New York Times*, London *Financial Times*, *Forbes*, *Fortune*, *Business Week*, and other business journals. Author of three books, he has consulted with numerous businesses concerning financing, operations, and strategic planning. Fred is past president of the International Business Brokers Association (IBBA), past chairman of M&A Source, a Certified Business Fellow, and past founding president of ACG-Utah.

A High School all-American, he went on to captain the Duke University football team, where the alumni specifically created a "Most Inspirational Player" award for him. Upon receiving his BA, Fred was drafted by the NY Jets but chose to pursue a business career.

Fred and his wife, Susan, live in Arizona, where he enjoys biking and working out five days a week, gardening and landscaping, genealogy research, and most importantly, spending quality time with Susan, ten children, and nineteen grandchildren. Fred and Susan are also active in the Church of Jesus Christ of Latter-day Saints.

"The Final Judgment is not just an evaluation of a sum total of good and evil acts—what we have done. It is an acknowledgment of the final effect of our acts and thoughts—what we have become."

— Dallin H. Oaks, 18th president of the Church of Jesus Christ of Latter-day Saints

www.ingramcontent.com/pod-product-compliance
Lightning Source LLC
Chambersburg PA
CBHW071749120626
46550CB00002B/728